The

Evergreen

Author

MASTER *the* ART *of*
BOOK MARKETING

Roseanne Cheng

with a foreword by Josie Robinson

[handwritten annotations:] Courses: — Pinterest course — Downloads $37 — Amazing Author Templates Platform Marketing ↓ $37 — $80 total for all

For permissions contact: roseanne@evergreenauthors.com

Paperback ISBN 13: 978-1-954108-00-4

Ebook ISBN: 978-1-954108-01-1

Printed in the United States of America First Printing: 2020

Cover design by Brigid Pearson

Interior layout and typesetting by Paul Nylander | Illustrada Design

www.evergreenauthors.com

For Dara and Amy, with all our gratitude

Author's Note: Throughout this book, I refer to authors I've worked with in the past. In order to protect their privacy and in the spirit of consolidation, I've taken liberties with both their stories and their identities.

The stories about my own missteps, however, are all true. Be gentle.

CONTENTS

FOREWORD

I'll never forget the first couple of years after self-publishing my book, because they were terrifying.

There I was, sitting with a warehouse filled with over 2,000 hardcover copies of the book I'd spent my entire savings to print—and no one was buying them.

Oh, and did I mention I'd also quit my day job to be an author full time so I had no other source of income? Yep. Those 2,000 hardcovers and the Kindle version of my book were it—so I needed to sell those books. Yesterday.

Yes, I believed in the message inside my book and knew it could help people. And yes, my main goal was and still is, to heal and inspire as many people as I can through my writing—but at that point in time all I cared about was selling those darn books as fast as I could because I had to feed my family.

How did I get to a place of having a warehouse full of books and no job? Well, let me backup a second and explain.

I had an extremely successful launch immediately after I released my book. The 1,000 hardcover copies I printed for my first edition sold out within a year of its release because people were buying stacks of the book to give as gifts (my book came out around the holidays which helped tremendously) and I was selling tons of books at speaking events. People loved it and were passing it from hand-to-hand organically.

So I thought to myself, "Wow! This is going so well! I should quit my super stable day job, print 2,000 copies for my next print run, and do this full-time because it's going to stay this way FOREVER."

Well, that didn't happen.

Once I made the decision to be an author "for real" everything came to a standstill. The holidays ended, the speaking gigs slowed down, and my sales stopped completely. It was me, a warehouse full of books that were costing me a fortune to store each month, and no safety net from a day job.

I started to feel desperate and began to spend hours each day obsessively googling "how to sell books fast" and did all the things the publishing gurus told me to like Goodreads giveaways, blog tours, book signings, weekly newsletters, etc, etc, etc. Then, I would head over to Amazon and check my rank to see if anything had changed. It hadn't. Nothing I did ever seemed to work.

At that point, I was *this close* to taking all those books and putting them into a landfill, and calling my boss to beg for my old job back. But I really, really, didn't want to do that. I wanted to find a way to sell my book, successfully and sustainably without selling my soul. So I went on a mission to find out how.

I decided to go outside the publishing industry to find the

answer, because the marketing advice I'd gotten there hadn't seemed to work for me. So, I started following and learning from people in technology and e-commerce who were selling things online (and hugely successful doing so) to learn how to sell my book.

What I learned from my deep dive into e-commerce is that there's a formula for selling things, and you can use it for pretty much anything—including books. I took the sales formula I kept seeing over and over again, and applied it to my book.

And that's when my sales took off.

I went from selling a few books here and there, to selling over 150+ books a month on Amazon alone. Plus, I started to get tons more traffic to my author website and people reaching out to me for speaking engagements or to be a guest on their podcast. I quickly sold out of those 2,000 hardcovers and created a print-on-demand version of the book so it would always be available. It felt like I went from chasing readers, to the complete opposite.

My author friends started to notice I was selling more books, and asked how I was doing it. I told them about the sales formula I had learned and started teaching it to them. Many of them saw jumps in their book sales, too.

I began getting calls from authors I didn't know asking if they could hire me as a marketing consultant—so I created an online course to teach them since I just didn't have the time to work with so many authors 17:1. Plus, I was repeating the same things over and over again, and a course seemed like a much more efficient way to share what I knew. (P.S. If you're interested in learning more about the course visit: evergreenauthors.com/masterclass.)

One of the very first students to enroll in my course was Roseanne Cheng. Little did I know that Roseanne would go from being my student, to becoming one of the best teachers I've ever had in my life.

At that time, Roseanne was working as the Marketing Director at Wise Ink, the indie publishing house I published my book through. Roseanne and I formed a friendship through Wise Ink and spent a lot of time talking about book marketing and sales because we were both helping so many authors with it.

Roseanne had some amazing success stories from the authors she worked with, and some tragic tales, too. I was fascinated with both, and would constantly ask her to share what she saw that was working to sell books, and what wasn't. She told me over and over again that the number one secret that separated successful authors from the ones who weren't was this:

> **Successful authors found a marketing approach that was authentic to who they are.**

The truth was, there were authors who got amazing results in my course. Authors who went from selling zero books, to making an extra $1,000 to $4,000 per month from their book sales as a direct result of the strategies they learned. But, there were also authors who didn't get those results.

Not even close. Even though they were using the exact same strategies, they weren't making any progress.

This drove me bonkers and I would spend hours working with these authors on different strategies to help boost their sales—but it didn't seem to make a difference. Thankfully, Roseanne stepped in when she saw I was heading towards a mega burnout situation and said my approach just wasn't going to work for every author. The best thing I could do for these authors, she said, was to help them find another marketing method that would work for them personally.

I admitted I probably wouldn't be able to help them find a different way since I was already "all in" on my own. Graciously, Roseanne offered to work with the authors who weren't getting results in my course to help them find a solution. Since she had worked on so many book marketing campaigns over the years, she had tons of firsthand experience to draw from and was familiar with every strategy under the sun.

So, we decided to join forces and that's how Evergreen Authors was born.

Now, we work with writers from every genre from all over the world to create custom marketing solutions for their books. We don't promote the latest book marketing fad or expensive gimmicks that game the NYT bestseller list—what we do offer is commonsense advice that we've learned over the years as working authors, and from other authors on the frontline of the publishing industry.

Our main goal is to give authors tools that help them free up their time to write, instead of spending any more wasted time on book marketing efforts that just don't work.

Roseanne and I have a *been there, done that* attitude when it comes to a lot of the book marketing trends we've seen over the years and hope to offer a more thoughtful, *evergreen,* approach for authors.

Again, it all comes back to finding the marketing strategy that works best for you and your book.

It was a game changer for me personally when I found the strategy that worked for me. And I've seen the same happen to the many authors we've worked with at Evergreen Authors who have found a strategy that worked best for them—it's like finding a goldmine in your backyard.

It's amazing to write and publish a book. That's something to celebrate, for sure. But to write and publish a book that people love to read and recommend to everyone they know, a book that gets amazing reviews and accolades, a book that propels you to bestseller status or being a leader in your niche . . . well, that's downright wonderful.

All of this is absolutely possible when you find the right marketing strategy.

Even if right now you have absolutely no sales and marketing experience and are feeling completely overwhelmed by where to begin, or, if you're a veteran who feels like you've already tried every book marketing tactic to no avail— I promise by the end of this book you will have a fresh perspective. And most importantly, you'll have a concrete plan of exactly what you can do to market and sell your book in the way that stays true to who you are.

Roseanne truly is gifted at helping people discover their book marketing genius zone. Don't think you have one? You do. This book is going to lead you to it, step-by-step.

Time to find your goldmine.

Josie Robinson
Cofounder of Evergreen Authors

INTRODUCTION

Congratulations! Your Work Is Just Beginning

Hello friends! Welcome to yet another book-marketing book.

In case I forget to tell you later, I'll start with this: Congratulations! You published a book!

A lot of people say they're going to write a book, and a lot of people write a book and never let it see the light of day, but not you! You did it! That's a big accomplishment, and something to be celebrated! If you need to take a few moments to pour yourself a glass of wine and really revel in the awesomeness of you for a bit, that's cool! Go for it! Come on back to this book when you're ready for some real talk, okay?

Because that's what this book is: real talk. It's not a pep talk about how to make it through the creative process, and it's definitely not a bunch of platitudes about just sticking it out and believing in yourself. This book is about *the work* of getting your book out into the wider world.

Here's the deal. Unless you're Stephen King, John Grisham,

or anyone else with an uber-famous name, or unless you're somehow the 1 in 1 BILLION unknown writers who just get super-duper lucky and see their book skyrocket to bestseller status, chances are that getting your book out there is going to take time, thought, and yes, a financial investment.

Wait, wait, don't leave just because I mentioned money!

Trust me, I understand you creative types—I am one of you! Bringing money into the creative process always sounded icky to me. A publicist? Yuck! Advertising? Double yuck.

I'm not a marketer, I can hear you saying. *I don't want to beg people on social media to buy my book. I don't want to sell my soul just to make a buck off my creative work.*

Amen to that. Here's where I come in. If you take nothing else from this book, take this: You do not need to do anything you don't want to do when it comes to book marketing.

I'm going to say it louder in case you missed it:

**You do not need to do anything you
don't want to do when it comes to book
marketing.**

But wait, you're probably thinking. *You said something about work. And money. I have to do* something, *right?*

Oh yes. You absolutely have to do *something.*

But you do not have to do anything that feels inorganic, too expensive, too overwhelming, not "you", or anything else just because someone says you have to. Liberating, right?

This was not something I "got" until my third book came

out, and I had been working as a marketing director for a publishing company for more than three years. That's right. I was an author myself, educating other authors about how to launch and sell their books, but it took *years* before I understood this basic, fundamental book-marketing principle:

Marketing your work in a way that feels fun and sustainable for YOU is the only way to go. It's the secret to success. It's the silver bullet we're all looking for.

Why did it take me so long to figure this out? Well, it was a few things. First, I fell into the trap of thinking that since I didn't have a marketing background, I should leave my marketing decisions for my book up to someone else, someone much smarter about such things than I was.

So I did what everyone told me to do:

- I hired a publicist.
- I blogged.
- I hosted events.
- I posted on social media three times a week.
- I hosted giveaways,
- I entered award contests.

My first two books were for kids, so this was *on top* of all of the classroom visits I was scheduling, book clubs I was attending, and teacher consults I was hosting. Have I mentioned I also had two babies at the time?

By the time my first book had been out in the world for a year, I was exhausted. Not just exhausted—what's a word for *so much more than exhausted*? Because that's what I was.

Don't get me wrong—I was selling books. But it was so much work. So. Much. Work. My work/life balance was gone. My creativity was gone. The joy of writing was gone. Then I started working with other, real authors—not the case studies I read about in a "best of" roundup on Twitter, but real people, like me. And I realized something really profound.

What works for one author doesn't always work for another.

This might seem like common knowledge to you, and as I write it, I think, *DUH*, but for me, at the time, it was pretty revelatory. Everything I'd read about book marketing used phrases like "foolproof formula" and "the only plan you'll ever need to sell books." It seemed to me that book marketing was very much a mathematical equation and a marketing plan involved checking off a lot of boxes.

But here's the thing: Creative work is not a mathematical equation. Sure, there is math involved, but there's plenty that cannot be quantified when it comes to getting your work out there.

- How do you account for people who love social media and people who hate it? The cost of participating isn't the same for everyone.
- How do you account for people who love public

speaking and sell their books at events and people who don't have any sort of speaking platform
at all? Or worse, hate public speaking in general?

- How do you account for the author who loves
blogging and the author who finds it to be a ter-
rible chore? The cost per hour of blogging isn't
the same there, either.

- How do you account for vastly different genres
and subgenres? How can you compare the success of a very niche nonfiction author who happens to ride a wave of a subject's popularity to
a very broad fiction author whose book is one
in thousands of books published every month?

- How do you account for an author who is mar-
ried with five kids and working two jobs and has
next to nothing to spend on marketing versus an
author who is retired and can spend hours per
day (and tons of cash) connecting with people
on social media?

The answer is: You can't. Even if you got a (likely small)
advance from a publisher for your book, I'm going to guess
that none of you wrote your book in the lap of luxury, with
no family, friend, or work obligations, or with any sort of
guarantee that your book would sell.

You wrote a book because the story mattered to you. You
had something to say, and you prioritized saying it. I say this
to authors all the time: Your book is an extension of you, not
the other way around. It's a damned miracle that any books

get written, ever, considering each of us has so much real life to live, am I right?

I quickly realized that working with authors means understanding what they love about their creative work, what gives them joy in connecting with their audience, what their individual budgets are, and most importantly, what they are willing to do on a sustainable basis for the lifetime of their writing career.

> **In other words, the book itself doesn't matter. What matters is figuring out what work you are willing to commit to doing to get your work out there, and then doing that work.**

So that's it, folks. That's the secret to book marketing. There's no magic formula. You need to figure out what works for you and do that. Once people get over the shock at how simple this whole thing is, they tend to be really relieved.

Wait, are you saying that I don't have to be on Facebook?

Yes, that's exactly what I'm saying.

So it's cool if I totally revamp my website and take down the blog I've been trying to get off the ground for years?

Sure can.

Amazon advertising is the only thing that sells books for me. It's okay if I JUST do that?

Absolutely. In fact, if it's the only thing that's working, why are you wasting time doing anything else?

The people who struggle most with this idea tend to be

the authors who are holding fast to their dreams of sitting on the beach, writing manuscripts, sitting for interviews with famous journalists, and watching the royalty checks pour in. **These are the people who are more attached to the dream of being famous than they are to the work of being a writer.** For those folks, the work of marketing feels like something they should be able to pay someone else to do for them.

I'll be honest—if you have this attitude AND wads of cash to spend on book marketing, feel free to put this book back on the shelf and call up the most expensive publicist you can find. Who knows? You might wind up on *The Today Show*! That's not the track I've gone on, so I really can't speak to how that might turn out for you. I will say that I have yet to see an author who has spent a ton of money on publicity be really, really happy with their experience.

So once we wrap our heads around this reality—that unless you're extremely rich, extremely lucky, or some combination of the two, you will likely not be catapulted into superstar status with your book—the dream itself comes into a bit more focus.

For me, and for the vast majority of authors I've worked with, the dream can be broken down like this: *I love writing and I want to write books. I want to sell those books to people who will find them educational and/or enjoyable. I want to make money off this endeavor. Lots of money would be great, but the money I make is secondary to the sense of accomplishment I'll feel knowing I've published a book I'm truly proud of.*

You'll notice throughout this book that I'm not at all interested in telling you to give up on your dream, whatever that looks like. What I *am* interested in is getting you to be honest about what that dream is and the work it will take to make that dream come true.

This book is for the author who is likely working a day job (or two), has a family and friends they like to spend time with, believes in their work but doesn't want to sell their soul to sell a few books, and is ready to get really focused on how they can get their work seen by their ideal readers.

No gimmicks. No creating a bunch of crap no one cares about. No follow-me-I'll-follow-you nonsense. No breaking the bank. No begging people on Twitter to buy your book. No forced participation in any sort of social media.

No doing anything you don't want to do.

I want you to keep this in mind as you read this book, okay? I have "Seven Steps" outlined here about how to be an "Evergreen Author" (more on this later). Within those seven steps, I'm going to throw out some ideas for you to consider and things I've seen work for other people in the past.

But if anything I say fills your stomach with dread, don't worry about it. Skip it. Likewise, if anything I suggest makes all kinds of light bulbs go off in your head, I want you to really listen to that and get excited about it.

By the end of this book, I want you to figure out at least two things you think you can commit to for the long haul, okay? That's it—two things.

Maybe you'll be inspired to take your love of Pinterest deeper and get to work on creating an ad strategy there.

Maybe you'll realize that your public speaking game needs work and you'll commit to getting better at it. Maybe you'll create an Instagram account. Or maybe you'll delete social media altogether. Maybe you'll revamp your website and make it a more interactive experience. Maybe you'll just write more.

What you choose doesn't matter. What matters is working from a place of *intention*.

Whatever strategy or strategies you choose for your writing career need to be *evergreen*, not a burst of energy or a quick jolt of excitement. Your strategy should be something that will be enjoyable, profitable, and sustainable for the long haul. That goes for the writing process, the platform building process, the sales process, the reflection process, all of it. Evergreen.

I co-founded Evergreen Authors with my dear friend and digital marketing mastermind Josie Robinson in 2019 because I want to help you create a *career* as a writer. An Evergreen Author isn't one who tries any and every marketing trick without putting serious thought and intention behind it. An Evergreen Author doesn't blow through their budget in a month with a publicist and come out on the other side with zero book sales and soul-crushing debt.

An Evergreen Author keeps their eye on the (realistic) prize, uses the information they gain from whatever plans they've implemented to make more informed decisions in the future, and most of all, focuses on action plans for getting their work out there in ways *that bring them joy.*

That's it — creative work that brings you *joy.*

Whether you're a first-time author or one who's been in the trenches for a while, I promise that this book isn't like other marketing books. You'll get a basic framework in the seven steps I've outlined about how to be an Evergreen Author, but how you choose to implement those steps is entirely up to you. You own this process, all of it, and that is really, really good news.

Ready? Me too. Let's go!

CHAPTER 1

Write and Produce a Really Great Book

I know what you're thinking. *Did I really just buy a book-marketing book that tells me the first step to being an Evergreen Author is to write a good book?*

Yes, you did. And before you roll your eyes and skip to the next chapter, I want you to hear me out on this.

I have always been told I am a good writer. I have memories of my eighth grade teacher, Mrs. Laiolo, telling me how talented I was, and how I should never give up on telling stories. Those accolades lasted well into college, where I could whip together an essay about Milton's use of light and dark as a motif in *Paradise Lost* in no time. A's came easily. Trigonometry? That's another story. But when it came to writing, I was *good.*

I wrote a bunch of stories and essays after college, some novel-length, some fiction, some nonfiction. I was doing what Malcolm Gladwell would call "putting in my 10,000 hours of practice." But it wasn't until I wrote my first published book, *The Take Back of Lincoln Junior High,* that I felt like I'd landed on something I wanted the world to see.

After dabbling with traditional publishing for a while, I decided to publish my book with Wise Ink Creative Publishing, an indie publishing house out of Minneapolis. My mentor and dear friend, Dara Beevas, connected me with an editor there for my book. And while I knew that she would probably find more than a couple misplaced commas (I'm bad about comma use, I admit it), I didn't think there would be anything she would want me to change in terms of the structure.

I certainly didn't think I would receive my line-edited manuscript with markings on every single sentence.

Every.
Single.
Sentence.

Turns out that I have some really annoying writing ticks that magically appear when I'm "in my creative zone." These include improper use of ellipses and dialogue tags; characters repeating the same lines over and over; and plot lines that just fizzle without resolution.

You can probably figure out where I'm going with this.

After some painstaking rounds of editing, I decided to have an illustrator draw a cover for me. I found this illustrator on the internet.

She had a great website. She was happy to work with me. Keep in mind that I'm not what someone would call a "visual artist." I don't have any opinion when it comes to decorating a home or a cake, or even having my clothes match, quite frankly. It's not my thing. So why did I think I could facilitate having a cover and interior for my book designed? It's a mystery.

I think you can figure out where I'm going with *this*, too.

Thankfully, Dara and the team at Wise Ink talked me off the ledge. They got me an amazing book cover, one that was nominated for a major award, and helped me see that I was going to destroy my chances of any sales before the book was even in print if I didn't leave the professional stuff to the professionals. (Thanks, guys.)

Don't get me wrong—the words of your book are exceedingly important. Before you do anything else, create a story or a draft that you feel is the very best you can make it. That will take time and effort, for sure. But I'm going to go out on a limb and assume that you, a writer, are not a professional in **all the skills you need to make a beautiful book**, okay?

When it comes to creating a really beautiful product, you need to make sure you have professionals behind you. Your book is a product, and you need to make sure it's as awesome as it can possibly be. Period.

But wait, there's more!

You might be tempted to skip to the next chapter at this point.

I get it. I need to get a professional cover for my book. Okay. I'm on it. This is advice every other book-marketing book gives, too, by the way. Next, please.

Right. Every author should know the importance of having a beautiful book cover. But an Evergreen Author knows there's a bit more to it than that.

Beyond the Book Cover

Okay, so you have a great manuscript. You have an awesome book cover. You have an interior designer who's going to make your book look beautiful on the inside. As far as the finished "product" goes, you've done the work, right?

Wrong.

I've observed many authors who check off those boxes and think, *Hooray! I'm done! Now I can start posting links on social media and making some cash!* But there is so much more to your finished product than the text and the cover.

An Evergreen Author looks at book publishing the same way they might think about purchasing a wedding ring. You don't just waltz into the first jewelry store you see, point at a ring, and take it home with you. You carefully measure it for size. You take a close look at its quality. You make sure it fits in your budget. You consider whether this is a ring you want to look at *for the rest of your lifetime.*

> **There should be a lot more intention behind the finished product than a great cover. Your finished product has many more facets to it.**

Don't believe me? Hop over to your favorite bookstore this afternoon and take a look at the books lining the shelves. You will notice the sizes and types of paper are all different. Some of the books are hardcover, some are soft. Some have embossing on the covers, some don't. Some have pages and pages of endorsements, some don't. Some are full color, some black and white, some include a gift with purchase, some are part of a three-part series. Do you see what I'm getting at here?

There are many marketing books out there that will tell you that Amazon's Kindle program is the only way to go. It's the fastest, cheapest way to publish, and it worked for others, so it should work for you, too.

There are also many marketing books out there which include horror stories of authors who have published through Kindle, been filled with regret, and wound up spending thousands of dollars with a boutique publishing house to get the book they wanted in the first place. And then you'll find horror stories of authors who have done *that* and gotten swindled.

Here's the deal: This whole author business, like any creative pursuit, is not for the faint of heart. It's work. But the good news is that we're not living in the times where only a select handful of white men got the opportunity to tell their stories. The advent of the Internet changed the game for creative artists. Your publishing choices are endless.

So no, there is no one-size-fits-all approach here. As I mentioned in the Introduction, the direction you take on your publishing path is very personal and has much less to do with what works for your genre than what works for *you.*

When I say this to first-time authors, I am almost always met with the same response: *But I don't know what I don't know! I don't even know the right questions to ask so I can make the best decision for me!*

Fair point. In the next section, I'll tell you exactly which questions to ask and what to do based on the answers.

The Evergreen Author's Guide to Production

Alright, here's the good stuff.

I want to first point out that if you're reading this book and already made book-production decisions that you might want to change or modify, it's often possible to do that, unless you've signed some sort of iron-clad contract with an agent or publisher. Making changes to an existing product can be a great way to give new life to an old book! So don't freak out if you read this section and think you've screwed your entire writing career up, okay? You haven't.

What all of this boils down to isn't books, but your personal goals. *My goal is to make oodles of money!* I hear that one all the time. Yes, of course. But if you're honest, is that *really* your goal? Would it be more accurate to say that your goal is to leave a legacy? Would it be more accurate to say that your goal is to build your business? Would it be more accurate to say your goal is to just try your hand at writing because you really, really enjoy telling stories?

Am I stumping you here? That's often the case when I work with authors. They will get really quiet and, maybe for the first time, get real with thinking through what their actual goals and expectations are.

"Making oodles of money" is something a novice writer would say, not an Evergreen Author. Yes, we all want to make money. We all want our books to sell. But for that to happen, you need to be making the right decisions around producing a book you're *proud of for your lifetime.*

You can start by asking yourself the following question:

Do I enjoy writing?

Wait, what? Are you serious? I wrote a book, for God's sake, of course I enjoy writing!

Really? I would say that of the hundreds of authors I've worked with, maybe half of them actually enjoyed writing their books. That's right. Fifty percent.

And this is a big deal, for one very important reason: If you don't enjoy the actual process of writing a book, chances are that this one you've cranked out is probably your first and last. That's okay! It just means that you will probably want to follow a different longterm, evergreen path than the person who really loves the process of writing. If that's you, I'll get to you in a minute.

If you, with all sincerity, imagine being the type of author who cranks out book after book **because you just really love writing,** I would recommend the following paths:

- If you're willing to put in the technical work, get smart on Amazon/KDP and self-publishing there. It costs literally thousands of dollars per book to self-publish with a quality indie publishing house, so if money is tight, Amazon/KDP is your best bet. It's cost effective, quick, and means you can write to your heart's content for the rest of your days. (We'll talk much more about finances in the next chapter.)
- If the thought of learning the technical side of publishing sounds worse than a double root canal, then you can do one of the following:
  - You can pitch your book to a literary agent and try to get a multiple book deal with a big-time publisher. There are many books out there about the pros and cons of traditional publishing and how to query an agent. For some authors, this is the best way to go, for any number of reasons. Just be prepared to wait . . . a lot. And understand that **just because you have a traditional publishing deal, it doesn't mean you don't have to do any marketing work. All the marketing work**

I talk about in this book still applies to you, whether you're traditionally published or not.

- You can partner up with an indie/hybrid publishing house. There are many out there that offer seriously amazing book services. Often, you can decide which services you'd like them to provide for you on an a-la-carte basis, and enter into a partnership with them that will allow you some flexibility (and maybe a cost benefit) for providing them with multiple manuscripts to publish.

See what I mean? If you love writing, you need to be thinking about how you can get your work out there consistently. I absolutely hate telling authors this, but it's true: You're starting a small business when you sell your creative work. You need to be a thoughtful business owner!

And how exactly do these options differ for the author who says, *I wrote a book I'm really proud of, but I can't say the process was really fun for me. I don't want to write more books. I just want this one to sell like hotcakes.*

The choices don't differ all that much, frankly, except for one important caveat.

If your book is the only book you ever publish, you might want to spend a little more time on making sure that it includes every bell and whistle you could ever want.

For example:

- You might want to splurge on hardcover copies, since it will be the only book that will "speak" for you. (For an author who wants to publish many books, this might not be cost-effective for the long term.)
- You might want to add contact information if your book is nonfiction, so you can use the book as an elevated business card for your business.
- You might want to be extra, extra careful when choosing your publishing partner, whether traditional or indie, and be sure that you're getting the highest quality editors and designers. (Yes, this is obviously true when it comes to more prolific writers, too, but when an author feels like their book is the only one they'll ever publish, they might want to splurge on a more boutique publishing experience knowing they won't have to make another investment like this again.)

I feel like I need to stop here and say that the most important thing you can do for yourself when deciding how to go about producing your book is to get *unemotional* about it. This is something I'll repeat a few times throughout this book because it's so important.

I get that this can be really hard to do, especially if you've written a very personal book, like a memoir. Sometimes authors stay in a really, really dark space for a long time after their books are finished, worrying that it isn't good enough to see the light of day. Sometimes authors are so trapped in their own creative headspace that they feel paralyzed when it comes to making logistical decisions for their books. They worry, *What if I make the wrong decision?*

I get it. Believe me. I've made plenty of wrong decisions on my own publishing journey, which I'll be sharing throughout this book. That's life. That's *especially* creative life.

You might choose to go the traditional publishing route, spend a year (or more) querying, and then come to the decision that a boutique indie publisher is the only way to go. You might sign with a publisher and see negotiations fall apart. You might go with an indie publishing house and encounter all sorts of hiccups you never could have anticipated.

The difference between an author and an Evergreen Author is this: An Evergreen Author is able to step back for moments of clarity and look at themselves and their work objectively. They're able to ask themselves the following questions:

> **What do I want my experience to look like? Why do I want my experience to look like that?**

If you can answer those two questions honestly, you'll find that your publishing options are really very simple.

Maybe you're thinking, *I want to be a famous writer and be featured in Oprah's Book Club.* Cool. Get thyself an agent, get a publishing contract with a major publisher, steel your patience, and make it happen. Maybe you're thinking, *I want to use my book to elevate my business.* Great! I highly suggest investing with a quality indie publishing house and getting a finished product that is absolutely beautiful and will really help your business stand out.

Maybe you're thinking, *I want to write a mystery series under a pen name and keep my day job as an accountant because I still have lots of bills to pay while I build my writing career.* Fantastic! Make sure you get a great cover. I think Amazon's cost-effective KDP platform is perfect for you.

Maybe you're thinking, *I'm not sure if I want to write more books. I'm open to any and all possibilities around publishing, but I'm anxious to see where this book takes me.* Awesome. Take it one moment at a time here. Get help with the aspects of publishing you need help with, and keep yourself rested, focused, and most of all, enjoying the process.

I know what you're thinking here: *How much is this going to cost me?* We'll get there in the next chapter, okay? First decide on what you value in the process, then we'll talk about what that value is actually going to cost.

Distribution

Please do not skip this section. I know you want to, because you think it's going to be boring. Honestly, it is a little boring, but I'm going to try to not make it boring. I'm also going to be brief.

Here's what you need to know about distribution:

**The way you publish your book
will impact how far and wide your
distribution reach will go.**

Most authors just pick the path of least resistance here by either doing whatever their publishing partner tells them to do regarding distribution or getting so impatient with the process that they just hurry up and slap their book up on Amazon/KDP because it's easier.

That's not a great strategy if you're looking for an Evergreen writing experience.

Here's what I mean: If your ultimate goal is to get your books into bookstores, simply putting your book on Amazon POD (Print on Demand) or printing at a place like LuLu is not necessarily the best option for you. Some bookstores will not stock your book if you've published this way. This is because they're unable to return the books that they purchase but that no one buys. In traditional publishing, bookstores are able to get a return on their investment by sending unsold books back to the distributor.

> **In other words, if you desperately want
> your book to be available in bookstores,
> you will want to publish through a more
> traditional publishing model, OR be sure
> that your self-published book is available
> via large wholesalers such as Ingram.**

There are major pros and cons to publishing your book with a major wholesaler as opposed to on your own through Amazon/KDP. I'll break them down for you.

Traditional Publishing

Pros	Cons
A contract! An agent who will help get your book into bookstores! Childhood dream come true!	People don't buy books in bookstores much anymore . . . why was this so important to you again?
In theory, you will have a marketing team able to help with getting your book featured in publications.	In practice, most traditional publishers will require the author to do most (if not all) of the marketing.
Someone else pays to have your book produced.	An agent and/or publisher will take a large percentage of your book sales.

Let me be crystal clear here: there is no "right" answer when it comes to this decision. The right answer is what works best for your goals.

Likewise, skipping the bookstore/wholesale route isn't for everyone. Here are some of the most obvious pros and cons for publishing exclusively online, with Amazon.

See what I mean? There isn't one way to publish your book. The route you choose depends on your goals for your Evergreen writing career, and not necessarily the genre of your book.

Publishing with Amazon

Pros	Cons
Publishing exclusively on Amazon/KDP is really cost effective. There is little financial risk and investment.	It's hard to get your book to stand out in the thousands of books that are published there every day.[*]
You can easily use a pen name and keep your professional and creative life very separate— ideal for romance and erotic fiction authors.	Publishing under a pen name can be an added challenge for those who want to grow an organic following.
You can run ads and lead people to your book on Amazon instead of relying on social media to constantly promote yourself.	For authors who really want to form lasting, long-term connections with their readers, this isn't ideal.
You can get printed copies of your book from Amazon at cost.	You are somewhat limited in your printing choices. We think Amazon/KDP works best for paperback books with black and white interior (like this one).

[*] We can help with that, though. Check out our masterclass, *Algorithm Alchemy*, at www.evergreenauthors.com.

The Bottom Line

Here's the bottom line, folks. We are living in this really, really cool time when you can have a writing career that works for your specific life and goals.

> **An Evergreen Author creates a really great book. Not a good book, not an okay book—a book they can stand by for their lifetime. An Evergreen Author makes informed decisions around the final product of their writing based on what they want their experience to look like.**

Focus on creating a book you can be genuinely proud of for the long term. Be intentional, ask questions, ask for help where you need it, and above all, create a book that you will be proud to show your friends, your family, your kids, and your grandkids. Nothing else will work if you haven't done this very important first step.

Chapter 1 Recap:

- Write a book you are proud of. Thou shalt do nothing if not this.
- Pick a publishing path that matches your goals.

CHAPTER 2

Wrap Your Head Around Finances

Oh no, money.

Oh yes, money. We need to talk about the money now.

The good news is that we're living in the golden age of publishing. You have so many options, options you should be considering with intention if you want to do this for the long term.

In the last chapter, we talked about how creating a quality book means really coming to terms with what you want your writing career to look like. That part of the Evergreen Author journey is the crucial first step to take before we start talking about money. Why? Well, let me give you an example.

I worked with an author once who poured her heart and soul into her self-help book. This wasn't just any self-help book—this was a memoir about an incredibly traumatic experience she'd been through. Writing that book had taken every ounce of her strength and courage. She planned to use that book to begin a speaking career, teaching educators how to approach young people who had been victims of violence.

In other words, this wasn't a fan-fiction book she wrote in her spare time. This book was her life's story, and an incredibly emotional piece of work. She wanted this book to elevate her career and really help with her ultimate goal of helping young people who had been through similar trauma.

At first, she pitched the books to agents. She got lots of rejections and then finally a bite. Then that agent sat on the book for years, unable to sell it, before finally ghosting her and leaving her back at square one.

Devastated, she decided she'd already wasted far too much time trying to continue to try to publish her book traditionally. She found someone online who was willing to format and publish her book for $1500. This seemed like a crazy good deal to her. She could have printed books in a matter of weeks. She was over the moon!

When the books arrived, she was slightly disappointed. She'd wanted a hardcover, but the person uploading her book said that wasn't possible. The cover design wasn't ideal, but the person she was working with assured her it was "fine." It wasn't what she'd envisioned, but she had books. That's what mattered!

Then she started booking her speaking events. She was told by bookstores that they couldn't carry her book because she had published on Createspace and didn't have it in wholesale distribution. She sold her book directly at events, and while this was okay, it was a logistical nightmare for her because it meant that she had to deal with money and shipping, something she knew other authors were doing, but had never wanted to do herself.

She had books. She was selling books. But she wasn't happy with the product, and the process of selling the book (for her) was exhausting.

Then the book reviews started getting posted.

It was hard to get past all the typos in the book.
I thought that the book was kinda unprofessional.
The author should really consider re-publishing this
  book so it fits her speaking business and brand more.

To say that this author was devastated would be an understatement. She was so upset over the whole process that she felt like she should cut her losses and quit writing. I couldn't blame her.

What went wrong here is the same thing that goes wrong for authors time and again. They don't do step one in the Evergreen Author process. They end up making publishing choices based on cost and convenience and **not the quality of the experience they want.**

Again, this is not about the book's content. If this author had come to me at the beginning and said, *Hey, I wrote a memoir about a totally crazy experience I had, I'm interested in publishing it as an ebook, and I don't want to do much more with it other than get it out there,* I might have said, *Okay, great, let's throw this up on Amazon and get it done quickly and painlessly. $1500 is a great deal!*

But this woman had *Evergreen* goals for her book. She wanted to use it to launch a career. If I had been working with her from the beginning, I would have advised her to invest in a much more quality experience, because the cost-benefit for her would be so much better in the long run.

I'm sure you can imagine, though, that this works both ways.

I have also worked with authors who've spent thousands (and thousands!) of dollars on a publishing experience they didn't want. They came into the process with a vision, were sold on a big, huge dream that wasn't their own, and were unable or unwilling to do the work required to make that dream come true. So their books sat in storage or in their basement for months, then years.

I genuinely don't want this for any author. This doesn't have to be you! Once you know what you want your final product to look like, we can move on to the work of building an Evergreen Author journey toward success.

How Much Is This Gonna Cost Me?

The answer to the question of cost depends on many different factors. Every author hates that answer, and I get it. I'm going to try to do this as simply and painlessly as possible.

If you've made it this far, you probably already know the major difference between indie and traditional publishing. But just in case, let me break it down quickly:

A traditional publishing contract means that your book will be funded entirely by the publisher, and they will keep

(a large percentage) of the proceeds from your sales. Finding an agent and a traditional publisher can be a long and difficult process.

Publishing independently means that you front all the costs of producing your book (which can be substantial, depending on your genre), and keep 100 percent of the proceeds from sales.

In recent years, there are many "hybrid" publishing companies popping up that offer a mix of the two publishing experiences.

When I talk with first-time authors about these options, they often will get overwhelmed. *There are too many options! I don't know which one is right for me!*

If you have gotten this far and haven't been able to wrap your head around your publishing path yet, **it's time to let your budget be your guide.**

Here are some different options based on your budget.

If you are broke as a joke, you have one of two options:

1. Learn how to self-publish on Amazon KDP. It's free to publish and straightforward. Your only cost will be getting your book profession-

ally edited and a quality cover designed, and
you can do this on the cheap if you set your
mind to it.

2. Start querying and get yourself an agent
and a traditional publishing contract so you
don't have to worry about upfront costs of
your book.

I recommend these paths for anyone who is in massive
debt of any kind. Why would you want to add to your financial stress?

I also recommend the traditional publishing option for
anyone who genuinely harbors any feelings that traditionally published books are "better" or "more legit" than self-
published books. If you really feel that way, don't "settle" for
self-publishing. Keep on querying and make your dreams
come true.

For the sake of time, from here forward I'm not going to
talk about pursuing a traditional publishing contract anymore. It's an option no matter what your budget is, and you
can always pursue that option down the road, even after
you've self-published. Let's focus on the self-publishing route.

If you have some cash that you're willing to part with to
make a quality product, you have two options:

1. Call around to some hybrid or indie publishing houses to see what sort of book package
you can get from them within your budget.

I recommend this for anyone who is technically challenged and needs help with the "business" side of things. I also recommend this for anyone who wants to feel like a part of a writing community, with professionals to bounce ideas off of. These prices can vary, as you'll see in the next section.

2. Build your book by hiring people — an amazing cover designer, an interior designer, editor, etc. — to do the publishing elements for you. I only recommend this option for people who are highly connected in the creative world and feel confident in their tech skills to put the pieces together to make a beautiful product.

Again, the first step on the Evergreen Author journey is creating a product you can stand behind for your lifetime. No matter how you put the book together, the process must result in a final product you love.

What about the Benjamins?

FINE! *Now* we can talk money. You'll see that pricing can vary WIDELY and depends on many factors. Again, the choices listed here assume you've chosen the indie publishing route. If you are querying agents and hoping for a publishing contract, you can skip to the next chapter or revisit this chapter if you change your mind.

THE DIY MODEL

Let's say you're one of those authors who has chosen to write for the sake of writing. You don't have huge, lofty goals of getting on the *New York Times* bestseller list, but you just love writing and want to have the option to keep cranking out books. And money is tight, so you don't want to spend a ton on this little creative venture you have going.

If you go the DIY self-publishing route for your run-of-the-mill paperback novel, you can expect to pay for editing, interior design, and an awesome cover. These prices will vary depending on how long your book is, but basically you will be paying something like this:

$1000-$3000 on content editing
$1000 or so on proofreading
$1000–$3000 on cover design (front, back, and spine)
$1000 or so on interior design

The DIY route means you're going to be hiring freelancers to do this work for you. There are pros and cons to this, as you can imagine. Some freelancers will charge by the word, while some will charge by the hour. Some will be cool with lots of back and forth, and others will have strict policies around how many times they will revise with you. Some freelancers are amazing, and others are not.

You will have to do a lot of research and be sure that you're making the right decisions as you build your book.

The DIY route also assumes that you, the author and now publisher, have some pretty extensive knowledge about how the publishing world works. You will need to know:

- How to upload your book onto Amazon yourself (otherwise, you'll have to hire it out).
- What formats and sizes your files need to be in (and how to manipulate those files if need be).

You might get the sense that I don't love this model, but you would be incorrect. I LOVE this option for the right author.

I once worked with a recent college graduate who was so excited to get started on her romance series and was really, really into the technical parts of publishing. She was young, resourceful, and ready to get her stories in front of readers. She just wanted to publish her work and see what happened with it. She also had very little to spend on her writing hobby.

For her, doing it DIY was the perfect option. She chose Amazon's Print on Demand model, so she didn't have to pay for a huge print run or house and ship books from her home, and she knew that her ideal readers would be downloading her books on Kindle anyway.

She's still selling books to this day!

However, I once worked with an absolutely wonderful gentleman who had been retired for more than 10 years and was on a fixed income. He had some crime novels sitting on his computer that he wanted to publish for his family and

friends. He didn't have any big plans to market the book—
he just wanted it out there.

You might think that I would recommend the DIY model
to him, too. After all, his book was a paperback and he didn't
have a ton of cash to spend. But I vehemently did not. While
he had a lot in common with the recent college graduate in
terms of budget and type of book, there was one very key
difference:

> **When I told this man that the cheapest
> option would also require him to
> have even the slightest technical
> knowledge, he looked at me like a
> deer in headlights. He had no interest
> in learning how to format his files for
> publication. He hated technology!
> And what if he had questions? Who
> would help him then?**

The DIY model wasn't right for him.

See what I'm saying here? I have seen too many authors
not be honest with themselves about what they're capable
of handling, only to be filled with regret that they didn't just
spend the money to publish well the first time.

The cheapest model is not necessarily the right model for
every author if they want an Evergreen writing career.

"The direction you take on your publishing path is very personal and has much less to do with what works for your genre than what works for you."

THE INDIE PUBLISHING HOUSE MODEL

With my first book, I went the traditional agent route first. I knew next to nothing about self-publishing, so I figured I'd try it out to see what happened. After some interest, lots of great feedback, and then ultimate rejection, I realized that if I wanted my book to see the light of day before I was an old lady, I would have to do it myself.

If you've taken one of my courses or watched my videos on the Evergreen Authors website, you've probably seen me refer to myself as "technologically challenged." My business partner, Josie, is the technical brains behind everything we do at Evergreen Authors.

I mean, don't get me wrong—I can do *some* stuff. But the honest truth is that for me, I would much, much, MUCH rather be creating content than figuring out how to make fancy sales funnels and lead pages. I don't want to spend my time learning how to convert Word docs to Mobi files. I don't really even know what that means.

Because I knew I wanted an *Evergreen career* as a writer, I went to an indie publishing house in Minneapolis called Wise Ink. I loved the women who led the company, I loved their mission, and most of all, **I loved being part of a group of writers I could go to for networking, ideas, and connections.**

Publishing with a small, boutique publishing house like Wise Ink means that you don't have to worry about building your book on your own. You're paying a company to make a beautiful product for you, plain and simple. For someone like me, who had absolutely NO desire to learn the technical side of publishing or spend time finding freelancers to create my cover and interior designs, this was absolutely the right decision.

If you decide to publish with an independent publishing house:

- For a paperback novel, you might expect to pay anywhere between $10k-$20k.
- For a hardcover book, you might expect to pay the same, plus another $5k for your hardcover print run.
- For a full-color interior book, such as a children's book or cookbook, tack on another $5k-$10k.

These costs do not include storage and shipping fees if you choose to have your book available at a wholesale distribution site.

If those numbers are giving you heart palpitations, keep this in mind: That price tag implies some **pretty stellar customer service**. For me, it included marketing brainstorming calls, access to informational classes held by the publisher, and networking within a private group of authors (one of whom would turn out to be my Evergreen Authors business partner, Josie!).

I also gave exactly ZERO thought to what my book cover and interior designs should look like, since Wise Ink worked with some of the best in the business, and did absolutely nothing technical to get my book into all the proper channels (not just Amazon, but bookstores and wholesalers as well).

I also made some of the best friendships of my life, and ultimately ended up working as the Marketing Director at Wise Ink for several years. Maybe those results aren't typical, but the point is **the indie publishing house route is an investment**, and not one to be entered into lightly.

THE HYBRID PUBLISHING MODEL

We're seeing hybrid publishing models pop up everywhere lately, and for good reason. What do you do for the author who knows they can't fully DIY their book, but also doesn't have the money to invest with a quality indie publishing house? You do something in between, of course!

The hybrid publishing model looks very similar to the indie publishing model, with one difference: **There is usually a profit-sharing element to the agreement**.

An indie publishing house will have you front the cost for the entire process and have you keep 100 percent of the proceeds of your sales, while a hybrid publishing house will have you pay, say, 50 percent of the upfront costs of production, and in turn you will keep 50 percent of your profits on the backend.

I have worked with several authors lately who have entered into this type of agreement and have felt like it was the best of both worlds. Yay!

My only word of caution here would be this: One of the biggest benefits of publishing independently is that you control your work—not just the book, but the marketing of the book for its lifetime.

You need to be very clear about who is funding the marketing of your book, and how that will work out for you, logistically, if you enter into a hybrid agreement.

For example, I worked with an author who entered into a contract with a hybrid publisher, got a beautiful book, and was ready to start running Amazon ads for it. She assumed that since her contract with her publisher had stated that they would split marketing costs 50/50, that the publisher would pay for half of those ads.

She didn't read the fine print. The publisher would only split the marketing costs if the author hired one of their very expensive in-house publicists. Not only was she on her own for her advertising campaign, but the hybrid publisher was able to pocket 50 percent of the profit from her work.

We're going to get to the marketing piece of all of this very soon, but until then keep this in mind: Being an Evergreen Author means having to try a few different marketing tactics and getting smart about building and growing your platform in a way that works for you. Many companies will offer "marketing support." You need to be 100 percent clear on what that means.

What about Marketing?

Yeah, what *about* marketing?

If you've gotten this far down the money pit, you're probably asking yourself, *Okay, great. I'm in for a few grand at least here if I want a really great book, right? Does that include marketing?*

In a word: No.

The rest of this book will be dedicated to the millions (okay, maybe not millions, but a lot) of marketing options you have for yourself and for your book. But until then, let's get this elephant out of the way:

> **How much should I be setting aside for book marketing?**

If you thought book publishing prices varied widely, you're about to be seriously shocked when I give you this answer: You can spend anything from ZERO dollars to ONE HUNDRED THOUSAND DOLLARS OR MORE on marketing.

Here's how an Evergreen Author decides on what their marketing budget should be:

1. **Gets it out of their head that, for the right price, they can pay someone to create a bestseller.** If you've thought this, stop it right now. I've seen many authors over the years fall into

this trap and each and every one has been
sorely disappointed. Much more on this later,
but the bottom line is: You've made it this far—
don't fall for gimmicks.

2. **Sits down with whomever they share finances
   with and makes a budget.** If you've already
   spent $10k on your book and you have to wait
   until next year to put any dollars into marketing,
   that's cool. If you have unlimited funds, you still
   want to put together a figure of what you think
   you can comfortably put aside for marketing.

3. **Decides on what efforts will bring joy and
   focuses on those efforts.** The rest of this book
   will be dedicated to helping you do that, but
   in the meantime, you can start wrapping your
   head around how much, financially, you're
   willing to put toward those efforts.

Before we move forward, it's time to put away any preconceived notions you have about how book marketing works.
My first book came out seven years ago—*light years ago* in
the publishing world. **Don't worry at this point about what
you think marketing should look like, what you do and don't
know about it, and how much any of it costs.**

We're going to talk about all of this in much more detail
throughout the rest of the book, but the bottom line is: Do
what you need to do to create a beautiful book first. THEN
worry about the marketing.

Cutting Corners

I would be remiss if I didn't add this little addendum because it's so very important.

I myself have fallen victim to cutting corners to save a few bucks.

Let's be honest here. The vast majority of authors approach their Evergreen careers like this:

> **I want a beautiful book, one I can be proud of for my lifetime. I'm willing to invest some money into it, but I'd like to invest as little as possible. Can't I do this both cheaply AND beautifully?**

The truth is that you probably can. Creative people are always looking for creative solutions for their work, and creative entrepreneurs are always coming up with new templates and ideas for authors to make book production happen more efficiently.

I just ask you, as an Evergreen Author, to approach everything with caution. Always read the fine print. Hire someone better than you to do the things you aren't good at.

Remember—sometimes you need to spend money to make money. Mistakes happen when authors are rushed and feel pressure. Be thoughtful and intentional about your publishing path and you'll be just fine. Promise.

"Do what you need to do to create a beautiful book first. THEN worry about the marketing."

Chapter 2 Recap:

- Choose your publishing path based on your goals and budget.
- Focus first on creating a beautiful book — THEN worry about marketing.

CHAPTER 3

Make a List of, Follow, and Connect with Authors You Admire

Can we talk marketing now, please?

Okay, fine. NOW we can talk marketing. Sort of.

It's very possible that you have blown through steps one and two of this Evergreen Author guide and know exactly what kind of writer you are and how you'd like your publishing experience to be. Yay! Good for you. You're ready to move forward on the Evergreen Author path!

If you're still doing some work on steps one and two, that's fine. Everything we talk about from here on out is going to help you understand how to take on the "business" side of getting your book out into the world in a way that will work for YOU.

You are welcome to do this marketing work at the same time as you finish your first book, or even before you start writing it. There's no "perfect time" to do this next step. In fact, once you start doing it, you'll realize you need to keep doing it throughout your writing career. It's going to become second nature. You're just going to be approaching this third step more from an Evergreen Author's perspective, with intention.

The Author Platform

Ever heard of the term "author platform"? It's one of those things when I work with authors that I can't assume they know before starting the marketing work. Your platform is what you personally will be using to sell books.

> **Your author platform consists of two elements: who you are and who you can reach.**

There are books upon books out there that will tell you how to build an author platform. At Evergreen Authors, we give talks about this *all the time*. We're going to talk about building your own author platform in the next chapter, but before we get there, I'm going to spend some time giving you some tough love.

I have no doubt your book is great. I'm sure it's unique and special and wonderful. Why would you go to all the trouble of publishing it if it weren't?

The pitfall I see authors fall into is thinking that their book, their work, and their image is so very unique that their path to publishing it will be its own, special path as well. So they start from scratch. They spend hours and hours on Pinterest looking at logo collections, cover images, and idea roundups for all the ways they can be connecting with their audience. Sometimes this can be fun—I do it myself! But sometimes it can be really overwhelming and discouraging, especially for a first-time author.

That's where this step in the Evergreen Author process comes in: You're going to take some time to watch and learn from the people who are doing it right.

Partnerships

I'm going to say this a lot, so get used to it: Creating lasting partnerships is the key to book sales. I repeat:

Creating lasting partnerships is the key to book sales.

First-time authors can tend to minimize the importance of partnerships. In their heads, they know that partnerships make sense. But in their hearts, they're thinking that once their book is published, it will somehow sprout wings and take flight all on its own.

Every now and then, a miracle will happen. Once in a blue moon, a completely unknown author will send out a tweet or create a website that is somehow noticed by someone who just happens to be connected to someone influential in their field, and a bulk order of 10,000 books takes place, and the author gets to sit back, relax, and revel in the joy of having done next to nothing to sell tons of books.

But the vast (and I mean VAST) majority of the time, authors need to spend time making serious connections in order to make those book sales happen.

How the heck does a first-time author do that?

You spend some time figuring out what other people in the business are doing.

You connect with those authors and influencers, connect with their connections, and create an organic network of people whom you can **watch, emulate, and learn from**.

So before you start sending out invoices for books, before you consider hiring a virtual assistant, before you get deep into the weeds of doing "book marketing stuff" for the sake of doing it, just take some time to research, watch, and connect with the people doing it right.

Who's Doing it Right?

Authors always get to this point and think, *Okay, cool. Watch and learn from the pros. Gotcha. So . . . who are the pros?*

Well, that's the thing. In order to answer that question, you'll have to go back to the introduction of this book and remind yourself that what works for one author doesn't always work for another.

This has nothing to do with your genre or your book. It has nothing to do with what your author friends are doing or what authors have done in the past. **It has everything to**

do with you being open-minded and curious when looking at how other authors are leveraging their platforms and connections.

For example, I worked with an author a few years ago who was bursting with energy and ready to make a splash with his book about education reform. He was totally inspired by all the teachers out there being hired as consultants, and had tons of fresh ideas about how to make public schools change for the better. He was ready to get his website going, get out there, and get to making the world better!

However, he quickly became overwhelmed by all the teachers out there in a similar space. There were so many books, so many teachers, so many administrators, all fighting to be seen on Twitter and Instagram, and they all seemed to be doing the same things. He couldn't quite figure out how to set himself apart.

Then he realized that connecting, following, and emulating other authors does not mean authors only in your genre.

While he still connected with other teachers on social media platforms, followed their accounts, and commented on their posts, he stumbled upon a cookbook author who was doing something a little different. This cookbook author was hosting a regular Q and A on her YouTube Channel, bringing on novice chefs and teaching them the basics of how to cook healthy dinners.

The author thought THIS was something he could get really excited about. Instead of bringing on novice chefs, he would bring on brand-new teachers to interview and mentor every week. He loved it, and it worked like a charm.

Similarly, I worked with a romance author who had formed a fast internet friendship with another author at the hybrid publishing house she was working with. That author wrote nonfiction self help, so they didn't exactly have much in common when it came to genre. However, this self-help author had an amazing "freebie" on his website—a downloadable mental-health checklist that was bringing him tons of traffic. The romance author realized that she could easily create a freebie for her website—a chapter from her book that never made it to publication.

When she did that, she saw her website hits triple. **All because she saw how other people were reaching people, and was open minded about that for her own work.**

And that's how it happens, folks. Seeing other people do something that seems exciting to you, and then making that work for yourself.

That's why you need to spend some time watching people who are further down the road from you, taking notes of what's working for them, and most importantly, being really honest with yourself about whether or not those tactics and strategies will work for you.

Don't Create Anything...Yet

This part of the Evergreen Author process is fun, if you allow it to be! Consider it your reconnaissance mission for figuring out what's going to best for you, whether you revamp a platform you already have running or begin creating one from scratch.

A word to the wise, however: Don't start creating anything yet. You're going to want to. You're going to get super excited by something you see another author doing, and then you're going to want to jump all over it and start creating.

I fall victim to this all the time. All. The. Time.

But by this point, you should know what I'm going to say about why this is a problem. An Evergreen Author is thoughtful and intentional with how they spend their time, resources, and money. Failing to do this can quickly result in wasted time and energy, as well as author burnout.

Start with the platforms you're already using, whether that's social media or something else. I've seen authors start with community forums, their local Rotary meetings, writers groups, professional groups, or even a quick Google search of something like, "writers in X genre."

Then start visiting websites. Sign up for email lists. Download freebies. Notice how these authors make themselves available to their readers. Notice the different platforms they make use of, some of them you might never have even heard of. Bookmark any websites that seem particularly cool to you for any reason.

My suggestion is to just keep a list, either in a journal or a Google doc. I keep my own list in the Notes app on my iPhone. My list looks something like this:

- Author Amy H. has a private group on Mighty
  Networks. She says it's a great way to offer 1:1

coaching without having to deal with social media. Look into Mighty Networks!
- Twitter chats to follow and participate in:
  - #satchat
  - #sunchat
  - #nt2t
- Author websites I love:
  - Judy Moody—love the playfulness and activities
  - Madeline Miller—love the simplicity and on-brand font choices
  - Russell Ricard—love the page devoted to good reviews of his book! I can do this!
- New content ideas:
  - Monthly creative writing prompt
  - NANOWRIMO activity guide
  - Greek Mythology unit on Teachers Pay Teachers
- Author Katherine Q. offers free 15 min consults— can I consider this?
- Take Melissa Griffyn's Pinfinite Growth course!

You'll notice that this is nothing fancy. It's just a bunch of notes for me to add to, consider, and grow from. Some authors will use Pinterest to create boards of people to follow and emulate. Others keep an Excel spreadsheet. It doesn't matter. Do whatever is easiest for you.

The point is, when it's time to start creating or updating your website, you will have your information consolidated in one place. And when you get overwhelmed with all the choices out there, you'll go back to this list to keep you focused.

Next, start connecting. Follow, comment, participate, get social. Don't overthink it. Don't participate in any "follow me and I'll follow you" silliness. Don't pay an expensive publicist or graphic designer to make connections for you. Just take some time to start connecting organically.

If you're a busy parent holding down two jobs and trying to create a writing career, maybe you do this for 10 minutes every other week. If you're able to carve out an hour on an early Saturday morning once a month, maybe that's the way to go. Maybe you get super into this and spend hours a day commenting on author posts, watching YouTube clips from other authors, and taking notes on blog post ideas. It's going to look different for every author. And that's a good thing! That is the BEST thing about being an author right now. The learning and connecting will be an ongoing process.

It's fun!

Connecting

Ah, the subtle art of connecting with authors, influencers, and anyone else you might admire and hope to leverage for your own financial gain. . . .

I could probably write a book on just THIS, am I right? I mean, a first-time author hoping to ride the coattails of someone else's success . . . what could possibly go wrong?

If you get nothing else from this chapter, I want it to be this: Starting your work connecting with and learning from other authors needs to begin and end in a place of ZERO expectations.

Zero. Expectations. None.

I'm going to tell you a couple stories here that break my heart, but they must be told as cautionary tales.

I worked with a man who wrote a fiction book about martial arts. He was SO EXCITED for this book and knew he had lots more books he wanted to write in the series. He also knew that he wanted to self-publish. He got into a contract with an amazing indie publisher in Texas who created a beautiful book for him. Steps one and two in the Evergreen Author process—complete! He was ready to shine.

When he started looking online at all of the potential partners he could have and all of the connections he could make and all the ways he could leverage other people's amazing ideas and platforms and make them his own, he was giddy with excitement. He was so inspired by all the people he saw who were taking their ideas to the next level. The ideas were flowing fast. He had lists of websites he loved, people he wanted to connect with, and groups he wanted to join.

True to form, this author had a lot of fun with this process. He loved Twitter and noticed a few great martial arts communities there, so he decided to go all in on that platform. He followed anyone and everyone who was in the martial arts community, both locally and nationally, as well as organizations he was interested in connecting with for speaking events.

Then he started engaging.

Keep in mind that this man had nothing but the best of intentions. He was in the process of creating his platform (which we will discuss in great detail in the next chapter), and it felt natural to him to jump in and start making friends.

Unfortunately, his "friendly outreach" was seen as spam.

Let me give you an example. This particular author found a Twitter chat to join that happened every Sunday afternoon. This chat was all about the latest in the martial arts community. It was a perfect place for him to meet and connect with people who were passionate about his subject matter, right?

However, instead of casually joining the chat and introducing himself, he said this: *I have a book coming out! You all will love it—here's the link to my new website! Preorder it today!*

He was shocked that there was no response. Everyone was so active on the chat—why wasn't anyone saying anything about his awesome book coming out?

If you don't see the issue with this, I'm going to refer you to book-marketing guru Tim Grahl. He taught me a lot about platform building. The most important takeaway is this:

Be relentlessly helpful.

Self-promotion is annoying. We're bombarded with it every day. When you're making connections, focus on **providing value** where you are.

That means no begging people to follow you. No asking for favors. No expectations.

As you build connections, start by being helpful. Share an

article you loved. Answer a question from someone in the group. That's it. No overthinking it.

Another cautionary tale I need to share involves an author I worked with who really admired a certain famous influencer in the cooking field. She knew that a connection with this woman would mean that her upcoming cookbook would land her on morning talk shows, viral Instagram posts, and bestseller lists.

In her mind, all she needed was to do exactly what this woman did, and she would be golden.

So she followed her on all her social media. She studied her website to see what she could emulate. She didn't look anywhere else but this one person, who was clearly doing something right.

Instead of picking and choosing pieces of the website that would work for her, she simply copied every bit of it. Same layout, same font, same everything. She started a YouTube channel even though she really didn't want to. She stopped blogging, even though that was the thing that got her started cooking in the first place and she really loved it.

By the time her book came out, she'd created a brand and persona that just wasn't her. She found her book to be a chore, not the passion project it had started as.

She was following a formula that worked for someone else, not a formula that would work for her.

The key word here is *authenticity*. The martial arts author came across like a smarmy salesperson and not an authentic partner with any of the people he was reaching out to. The cookbook author was taking on a personality that

"Connect with authors, influencers, and their connections, to create a network of people you can watch, emulate, and learn from."

wasn't hers. There's only so long a person can do that before burning out.

I can't tell you what the right answer is for you. What I will say is that when you're in the midst of Step 3 in the Evergreen Author process, you will want to keep reminding yourself that you do not *need* to do anything another author is doing.

Listen to your gut. Take your time and be patient.

Remember, this is a long game and not a sprint. Don't react emotionally to something cool you see another author doing on their website or social media. Take the time to think about why it works and how it could work for you.

Chapter 3 Recap:

- Take the time to learn from people who are using their platforms in unique ways and decide if there are any elements you think you could emulate.
- Start connecting with people from a place of ZERO expectations. The best partnerships will come when you are sure of who you are as an author and what you can bring to the table.

CHAPTER 4

Create Your Author Platform

There's that P-word again — platform.

Josie and I talk about author platforms all the time. It's one of our favorite subjects. In fact, if you head over to our website at Evergreen Authors, you can find a webinar where we give our signature talk about how we feel about creating a great author platform.

Why do we love talking about author platforms? Well, mainly because it's such a misunderstood part of the author process.

Authors often mistakenly think that their author platform is their Facebook page or any other form of social media. Or they think their platform *needs* to look and feel a certain way.

Your author platform can contain many different elements, including social media, your email list, your speaking business, and anything else you are doing or plan to do to get your work out into the world. But the truth is, each author's platform is going to be unique to them.

Again, your personal author platform is a combination of who you are and who you can reach.

I mentioned this in the last chapter because in studying what other authors are doing "right" that's exactly what you're doing — studying other authors' platforms. You're seeing what's working for them and how you can incorporate those elements into your own career.

You're piecing together a platform that will work for you.

No, there is no "one way" to do this. If there were, we'd love to share that secret with you. If platform building were a checklist of things you could do to ensure bestseller status, we would simply give you that checklist here and call it a day. But that's not how any of this works, and that's a good thing. It means that you get to decide how to take who you are and who you can reach to whatever level you choose to.

In figuring out who you are (Step 1 in the Evergreen Author process) and in being inspired by others who are reaching their audiences in different ways (Steps 2 and 3 in the Evergreen Author process), you can move on to the fun work of Step 4 — figuring out how to create a platform that is sustainable for YOU and successful for the long term.

The 80/20 Rule

The book that changed the game for us at Evergreen Authors is *80/20 Sales and Marketing* by Perry Marshall. It blew the lid off the idea that we should all be doing the same marketing tactics to sell books.

The premise centers around the Pareto Principle, which states: 80 percent of your sales come from 20 percent of your efforts.

In other words, the vast majority of your sales will come from a few strategic things you do.

This is why we advise that you take some time figuring out what kind of writer you are, what kind of publishing path makes sense for you, and who is doing things "right" from your perspective. No more trying anything and everything to see what sticks. No more wasting money on expensive publicists who promise you the world and never deliver.

The key to applying the Pareto Principle to your book marketing work is simple: **Figure out a couple things you're willing to do and go all in on those things.**

Platform Must-Haves

One of our masterclasses at Evergreen Authors, Book Launch Blueprint, goes into great detail about all the different options you have for building your author platform. If you feel confident that you're ready to start taking some of the inspiration you've found in Step 3 and are ready to start creating, that course might be perfect for you.

One of the things we mention in the course is that while everyone's author platform is going to look really different, there are two things that most every author will "need" in setting up their platform.

Wait, didn't you say that I didn't "need" to do anything I didn't want to do?

Yes, I did, but hear me out. I consider these two items as essential as a toothbrush and toothpaste on a vacation. They are the basic building blocks to setting up your career as an Evergreen Author. They can be as simple or as complex as you'd like to make them, so relax, okay? Everything *else* is up to you.

The Two Essential Components of Your Author Platform

The way I see it, there are two things every author (and small-business owner) must have in order to establish a platform:

A website and an email list.

That's it. Those two things.

Lucky for you, you're following the Evergreen Author philosophy around marketing, which means that by now you've already done some work looking at other authors, even authors outside your genre, who are doing this right.

And more importantly, you've done some reflecting on what things you think you'd feel comfortable taking with you on your platform building journey, and what things you would never in a million years waste your time on.

This means that your website and email list, these two essential components of your platform, become really simple.

1. **Create a website that showcases your book in some way.** Your website should be a landing page—a place anyone can go to find out more about you and your books. There are zillions of different ways you can create this, as you know from your work looking at other authors and influencers in Step 3. You can make it something you update constantly or something you never have to touch, ever. You can make it a place to sell books or you can make it a place to house all the links to the places your book is available. How you create your website has more to do with the effort you want to put into it rather than the genre you're writing in. Have fun with this! Hire it out to a professional if you don't have web-building skills.

2. **Create an email list of people who are interested in your book.** Like your website, this email list can be simple or complex. Your email list can be something you use once a month or once a year. If you're starting at ground zero with no email addresses, that's totally fine. The point is to start using email to connect with people as the author that you are. No more sending blast emails out from your Gmail account—it's time to get professional!

For much, much, much, MUCH more on these two essential components of your author platform, you can visit our Book Launch Blueprint course at our website, EvergreenAuthors.com. It will take you step by step through all the ways you can create these two components, as well as offer tons of examples of inspirational authors.

Who You Are and Who You Can Reach

I've just told you the two things you must have in order to create an author platform: your website and email list. I'm hoping you feel comfortable moving forward into the myriad other options you have getting your work out into the world.

Remember how I said earlier that your author platform is a combination of **who you are and who you can reach?**

Well, each author is going to be very different here, and again, it has much less to do with genre and more to do with who you are and what work you're willing to put in.

Do yourself a favor before reading more and repeat this mantra:

> *I do not have to do any of these optional platform ideas. These are just suggestions. An Evergreen Author is honest about their capacity to do things. I will not commit to doing things just because someone else did them. I'll only commit to doing things that will fill me with joy.*

66

Got it? You can write this on a Post-It note and keep it by your mirror, set it as your ringtone, I don't care — just don't forget it.

These platform ideas are optional because they are, in fact, *choices* you are going to make moving forward into your marketing work. Each and every author is going to make different choices based on who they are and who they are able to reach.

Let's start with the first element of your author platform: *who you are.*

This isn't some sort of existential question, so relax. "Who you are" centers around the credentials behind your name.

Credentials? I don't have credentials!

Yes, you do. Don't get me wrong. If you're a nonfiction author, the "who you are" piece of your platform is more important than it is for a fiction author. Are you a baker? A teacher? A creative writer? A doctor? A parent? A combination of a few of those things? If you're a fiction author, you're not off the hook. Are you a lover of your genre? Are you someone who's always been a creative writer?

In other words, what gave you the authority (get it, AUTHORity?) to write a book in the first place? That's what I mean when I say "credentials".

I've found that some people, mostly women, undervalue their expertise, talent, and experience when they talk about their creative work.

Me? they say. *Oh gosh, I'm not really a writer. I just play around with poetry and well, you know, I'm just sorta trying this whole thing out and it's probably not going to go anywhere but I'm having fun . . .*

Stop that right now. I mean it. RIGHT NOW. An Evergreen Author owns exactly who they are and what gave them the confidence to write a book in the first place.

Why is this so important? Here's why:

Being an Evergreen Author means you have to be confident in your skills. You're creating a career around your book. Maybe it won't pay all the bills, at least at first, but you wouldn't start teaching and tell people, "Well, I won't really consider myself a teacher until I make X amount of money." And you wouldn't hold your newborn baby and say, "I'm not actually a parent until my child goes off to college."

You are a writer *now*, and you've written something you believe in so much that you're willing to put it out into the world. (If this isn't true for you, go back to Step One, please.) Get excited about your accomplishment so other people can get excited about it, too.

Okay? Got it?

When we talk about embracing "who you are" at Evergreen Authors, what we're really doing is setting a framework for your communication about your book, no matter what that ends up looking like for you, and getting rid of anything extraneous that might get in the way of that message.

This is why getting clear on "who you are" is the first step in the platform-building process. Everything you do from this point on will be a direct result of getting real with the part of you that you want to put out into the world.

For example, I write fiction for high school English

teachers. When I talk about my book, when I create professional relationships, I always lead with that. Not the fact that I'm a mom, not the fact that I love yoga, not the fact I can speak a little Mandarin after living in China for three years (which is true!).

So when I think about building my website, I think about it in terms of it showcasing the "who I am" that really matters—my teaching experience. When I create marketing materials, I do so with teachers in mind. I speak directly to my audience, whether that's on a social media account, a blog post, or even in a business card I have made.

My business partner, Josie, writes inspirational self-help books about gratitude. Her website doesn't include her accomplishments as a high school guidance counselor and it doesn't include a list of her favorite vegan recipes. Everything on her website is about self help, and gratitude.

At Evergreen Authors we call this the "bumper sticker test". The "who you are" that is the "AUTHORity" should shine bright and should be obvious and apparent after one click on your website.

Fiction authors—this goes for you, too. I've seen fiction authors have incredible websites where they showcase their book covers, create creative blog posts, connect with other fiction writing groups, and share their expertise about writing. Some websites are really interactive, some aren't.

As with all of this work, how you showcase who you are is entirely up to you. It can and will grow and change. That's the best news of all.

Next, we move on to who you can reach.

Of all the pieces of the publishing journey, the question of who exactly you can reach is the trickiest. For example, just because you're a home chef doesn't mean you have the same reach as Ina Garten. And just because you wrote a children's book doesn't mean you have access to thousands of story-times every day.

Not everyone has the same reach, at least not at first. But then again, maybe your reach is more than you realize. Maybe your book is **the direct result of the people you've been reaching for quite some time now.** (This is often the case for nonfiction authors.) Maybe you've built a huge Instagram following over the years. Maybe you've already created a speaking career, or maybe you HOPE to create a speaking career (and in the last step started following and connecting with other authors who have done it right).

For me, realizing who I could reach as an educator was a game changer. When I sat down and really thought about how many school connections I had, how many teacher conferences I knew about, and how I could use my skills as a teacher to help build a business around being an author, I knew instantly that I didn't need an agent or a big publisher to sell my book. I could do it myself. Those connections set me up for a writing career that has lasted for years and is still going strong.

You might be able to easily figure out who you can reach or you might need to think on it for a while. You might have a pages-long list of who you can reach already or you might have one or two names. It doesn't matter where you're starting. What matters is understanding that **cultivating this element of your platform and consistently growing the list of people who you can reach IS the work of book marketing.** It's a process and a journey, one that ends only when you stop putting in the work.

Here's what sets an Evergreen Author apart from an author who isn't in this for the long journey:

> **An Evergreen Author takes their author platform — who they are and who they can reach — and gets laser focused on reaching the people who will benefit from their work.**

That's it. That's the secret to 80/20 Marketing or applying the Pareto principle to your marketing work.

But how do you do that?

You stay realistic and have fun getting creative, which is what we're going to talk about in the next section.

Optional Platform Ideas

This might be my favorite section of the book. I absolutely love sharing stories of real authors who have gotten creative with their platforms and sold books in unique ways. More than that, I love it when authors realize just how simple it is to apply the Pareto Principle to their author career.

But before going forward, I want you to remember the most important element of all of this marketing work: JOY. Creative work that brings you joy. Got it? Good.

I worked with an author once who wrote a diet and exercise book for senior citizens. She herself was retired, and when she did a lot of reflecting on who she was and who she could reach, she realized two important things about her author platform:

1. She didn't want to do social media. She simply couldn't be bothered to learn it. (Her ideal readers weren't using it much anyway—why should she waste her time?)
2. She loved (and I mean LOVED) speaking in front of groups. It brought her the most joy.

So when we sat down and talked about her Evergreen Author platform, here's what she decided to do:

1. Create a great website and get started on an email list. (Obviously.)
2. Make a list of each and every senior center in her home state and the state she usually spent summers in.
3. Reach out to each of those senior centers with a personal pitch to come and speak. Her speaking fee included a copy of her book for everyone in attendance.

As far as I know, this author is still going strong using this simple strategy. Could she do more? Sure! But she doesn't want to. Plus, what she's doing is selling books and bringing her joy.

> **She took who she was and who she could reach, and then got honest and committed to doing the work of reaching her ideal audience. That's an Evergreen Author.**

I also worked with an author who created an absolutely phenomenal group on Facebook around the difficult topic of bereavement. This woman was reaching thousands (and thousands!) of people with each and every post she made, with tons of organic engagement. By the time her book came out, she did a couple updates to her website so she could sell books from there, but when it came to doing anything outside of Facebook, the answer was a resounding no. All of her focus was on Facebook, where she was already reaching people. She took what she was already doing and amplified it to sell books. That's an Evergreen Author.

I worked with a fiction author who, as a first-time writer, was starting from scratch. After creating his website and starting his email list, he tried his hand at a few things to see what felt right for him:

1. He blogged
2. He created a Pinterest page

3. He created an Instagram account
4. He created a Twitter account
5. He created a Facebook page
6. He learned how to create Amazon ads

After a couple of months, he realized he hated blogging, so he scrapped it. Same with Pinterest and Instagram—his readers just weren't there. Twitter was active for him and he loved engaging with people there, so he kept that. He also really loved playing around on Facebook, so he kept that, too.

But the thing that really worked for him was Amazon advertising, which he learned by taking our Algorithm Alchemy course at Evergreen Authors. So while he spent time on other, optional elements of his platform that brought him joy, he went "all in" on advertising on Amazon so he could maximize his book sales.

He took who he was and who he could reach and made a plan to try some things that sounded good to him. After giving it a go, he quit doing the things that didn't bring him joy and focused on the things that were the most effective for selling books. That's an Evergreen Author.

One of my favorite authors I've worked with was a consultant who wrote a workbook for HR professionals. He was active on a bunch of different platforms and was reaching people wherever he went. He didn't quite know what to choose when it came to going "all in," since he was really a master at creating community wherever he went.

After reflecting on this, he realized that publishing a book meant he had a chance to reimagine how he put

"Figure out a couple things you're willing to do, and go all in on those things."

himself out there. He took advantage of the opportunity to create boundaries around his social media accounts, something he'd been wanting to do for some time. He decided to focus all of his author marketing work on his LinkedIn profile and make his other accounts private and personal. He learned how to run LinkedIn ads and even hired a virtual assistant to help him create content there. That's an Evergreen Author.

Will there be trial and error when it comes to figuring out the optional platforms that you want to engage in? Undoubtedly! But I want you to notice something about these four very different authors: None of them were doing more than a few things at a time. None of them were trying to be someone they weren't. None of them were doing something just because someone else was doing it. They tried things strategically, got really honest really quickly about what worked for them, and then focused on those things.

Need some more ideas? I've seen authors use any number of these things with wild success:

- Pitching to hospitals
- Pitching to yoga studios
- Mass mailings
- YouTube
- Etsy
- Pinterest
- Blog tours
- Teachers Pay Teachers
- Event hosting

- Presentations at cooperative workplaces
- Instagram Stories
- Digital downloads
- Facebook Live events
- Book clubs
- Print magazine advertising
- Keynote speeches
- Holiday Buy-One-Get-One (BOGO) offers
- Subscription boxes
- Quora
- Medium
- Pitching Op-Eds to newspapers

Important note: This is not a checklist. No one is going to have success doing ALL these things.

This also isn't a mathematical equation. Sometimes a platform you get excited about doesn't resonate the way you thought it would. Sometimes a platform you don't give any thought to at first ends up being the key to book sales. (Side note: I still kick myself for not engaging on Pinterest earlier in my publishing journey. That platform would have been perfect for me as a teacher at the very start of my author career, and I really enjoy it there! Sigh.) **It's a matter of figuring out where your readers are and meeting them there in a way that's sustainable and enjoyable for YOU.**

The good news is that if you're reading this book and realizing you're doing too much or not enough, you can always course correct. As an Evergreen Author, that's what you do. You don't just throw your hands in the air and say, "Forget it! This just isn't for me!" You find something that works for you and keep learning.

The other good news is that you have plenty of options for trying out these platform ideas, no matter what your budget or experience. If you need help with pitching yourself, head over to Evergreen Authors for a couple resources on how to do that well. If you need help with content creation, hire an intern or a virtual assistant. If you need to take a break, take it. If you need to learn how to do something better on any of your chosen platforms, learn it. If you hate doing any of this, stop doing it and find something you like better.

That's it, folks. Get started creating a platform that brings you joy.

Automation

We need to talk about automation.

I once worked with an author who was the epitome of an Evergreen Author:

- Awesome book: check
- Publishing plan: check
- Finances figured out: check
- Fun and sustainable platform: double check

What do I mean by "double check"? Well, this author wrote children's books, and she was all in on a platform that she knew was going to bring her joy. She was an active blogger, excellent on Facebook, and used Pinterest religiously. Her audience grew organically every day and she absolutely loved it.

We'd talked about automation before, but it was always something that didn't seem to take priority for her.

> *I love being on Facebook during the day — I don't need to schedule any posts!*
>
> *My Sunday mornings have always been spent writing my weekly blog posts, and I just post them as I write them. So easy!*
>
> *Pinterest is so much fun for me. I don't need to automate anything — I just hop on a couple times a day and start pinning.*

For a long time, this worked great for her. Her books were selling and she was totally enjoying herself. Awesome!

And then life happened.

Her mother got very ill, very quickly. In a matter of a month, she went from being a single woman with a really fun hobby she loved to being a full-time caregiver who hardly had enough time after work to brush her teeth, let alone hop on Pinterest and pin fun posts from other children's book authors.

Not surprisingly, her book sales went from steady and secure to absolutely nothing. Zero.

When we're talking about building a sustainable platform, this is what we're

talking about: A platform that can run for you, automatically, even when you can't be there.

How to Automate Your Author Platform(s)

Part of going "all in" on a platform is learning how to make it run without you having to be chained to it 24/7. This means figuring out how to use a scheduling tool that will work for you.

Does scheduling your posts and content mean that you'll never have to hop on Facebook or touch your Amazon ads again? Of course not. Social media is social. You will absolutely need to check, monitor, and respond to people there. These platforms require your consistent engagement. Amazon ads (or any targeted advertising) is inherently automated, but you'll still need to check, finesse, and restructure your ads based on the data you get.

But there are ways to take the reins on your platform by getting real with the amount of time you're able to invest and thinking ahead, as much as possible, to the content you're willing to create to engage people.

In the marketing world, this is called a **content calendar.** I've seen very complicated versions of these, including three to five social media posts *per day*, across multiple platforms. If you have the resources and desire to make that sort of commitment, go right ahead! But for the average Evergreen Author, there's probably not the energy or time for that.

When we talk about creating a content calendar at Evergreen Authors, all we're saying is to first decide on the platform(s) you're willing to engage on and make a plan for how you're going to do two things:

- Create original content there
- Respond to comments and the content of the people you are connected to

That's it.

Keep in mind that not all platforms are created equal (which is of course why you've already done your homework and gotten really intentional with the platforms you've chosen).But other than creating content and responding to content, there are no rules around how "much" you have to do on any platform.

You can post, email, and share as often or as little as you like. The focus should be on providing value, which we'll talk about in the next section.

Quality over quantity, ALWAYS.

Quality Content

This is another topic I could probably dedicate a whole book to. Conventional wisdom will have you think that you need to be posting content on social media all the time in order to be seen. This is simply not true.

As an Evergreen Author, you're going to be posting

content—whatever and WHEREVER that means to you—in ways that are "relentlessly helpful."

Will you be letting people know about your book? Will you be making sure people know about upcoming deals and promotions, and how to contact you? Of course! But that's not the core of what you'll be doing. Putting yourself out there in a way that feels good for you is going to involve putting yourself in the mind of your ideal reader and giving them what you think they might want from you.

What this means is that you're creating your content in two ways:

The first is your core content. Your core content consists of blog posts, links, emails, etc., which you carefully plan out before you post as part of a strategic effort to draw people to your book. For the average Evergreen Author, we recommend connecting with your audience once a month. That's 12 times per year. One fiction author/blogger we worked with mapped it out this way:

- January Post: New Year's Writing Resolutions
- February Post: Authors I Love
- March Post: Goodreads Spring Roundup
- April Post: Spring Sale on My Book Series
- May Post: Bookish Gifts for Mom for Mother's Day
- June Post: Summer Reading List
- July Post: Summer Writing Recap
- August Post: Fall Books I Can't Wait to Read
- September Post: Incorporating Reading into Your Back-to-School Routine

- October Post: Progress on My Next Book!
- November Post: Gratitude/Thanksgiving Sale
- December Post: Free Shipping Holiday Sale

This particular author was active on two platforms: her email list and Facebook. So to make it easy, she simply created the email to send to her subscribers and then cross-posted the content to her Facebook page. In November and December, when she was running sales on her book, she boosted those posts with ad dollars.

That's it. A year of content.

When I tell people this is all they need to do, they tend to look at me like there's some sort of catch.

Wait, shouldn't I be doing more than this? Twelve posts a year? That can't be right.

Yep, it's right. Because remember, these posts will be relevant across any platform you're choosing, and even some platforms you haven't thought of yet.

Shouldn't I be creating content specific to certain platforms I'm using?

Sure, but I never recommend reinventing the wheel if you don't have to. If you're working on two very different platforms, you can take the same core content and just modify it to make it work for that platform.

Stop making this so hard on yourself, okay? Because here's where it gets awesome:

You can create this content anytime and then schedule it.

The fiction author I just mentioned is a teacher with three young children. She doesn't have time to be blogging and creating new content during the week and often her weekends are filled to the brim with kids' activities. So she just sets aside an early Saturday morning once every month while the kids are sleeping and cranks out her core content for the next month or so. Then she hops onto her blog and schedules her posts there. And she hops onto Facebook and schedules the same posts there.

If she has time, she will sometimes squeeze in an ad campaign on Pinterest. She's really dynamic in person, so I've been wanting her to consider cross-posting to a YouTube channel to see if she can connect with people that way. Maybe someday. But for the most part, she just sets her posts and then forgets them.

There are ways you can do this in one large scheduler, like Buffer, however I recommend that if you're only using one or two platforms, you use the scheduler within the app (if one is available). I'll explain why in the next section.

The author I just told you about has been writing for years and is on her seventh book. She enjoys consistent engagement and sales, and is never stressed about doing more than what she's capable of. That's an Evergreen Author.

The second type of content is your connection content. These are the ways in which you are engaging with the audience you've established. For the average Evergreen Author, I recommend hopping onto your chosen platforms once or twice a week to be sure you are responding to emails, answering questions on your social media pages, and reaching out to the people you've networked with and followed.

I work with a nonfiction author who, like the fiction author I just talked about, had a core content strategy that he was using on LinkedIn. His core content was posted the first Monday of every month with the help of his virtual assistant and was very specific to whatever was happening in the news at that specific moment. So while he didn't have the luxury of planning out a year of specific content (he obviously had no idea what the top news stories of the month would be in advance, not to mention LinkedIn doesn't have a scheduling tool within its app to date), he did have the ability to structure a monthly roundup that he could allocate time for and have his assistant do for him.

His LinkedIn platform was extremely active. It was very much a part of his brand and extremely important to his business that he be responsive. So that meant that he needed to take some time every day to just hop on LinkedIn and scan through his notifications and direct messages to be sure he was responding, or at the very least "liking," his replies.

Isn't it common knowledge that we should be responding to people's posts and emails? Do I really need to account for time to do this as an author?

Absolutely, 100 percent yes. Here's why: Engaging in a platform, especially a social media platform, means that you need to be all in. Social media is social, so be social! If you've chosen a platform like Twitter or Instagram or Pinterest, the biggest mistake I see authors make is to throw content out there, not log in for weeks and months at a time, and then be shocked when their posts aren't getting seen.

Here's the deal with social media—those "free" platforms you're using aren't free, not really. Besides selling your data, they're also scouting out and rewarding the people who are using the platforms to their full advantage. That means advertising on them, scheduling content on them, and responding to other people on them.

This is why we tell authors to pick one or two platforms and go all in. It's unrealistic to think you can learn all the social media platforms and keep up with all their (constant!) updates and changes.

Pick one or two platforms where your readers are and where you like hanging out, and go all in: Comment. Like. Respond. Share. Take the time to do for others what you would like done for you!

What If I Don't Want to Be on Social Media?

Trust me, I'm not here to tell you that you MUST be on social media to sell books. I spend time talking about those platforms because they can be very effective at growing an audience. But you do not in any way need to be there.

Does that mean you don't need to be creating content?

No. It just means your platform's content isn't solely made of social media posts and blogs.

I'm using the word "content" pretty loosely here. Content that's not social media includes:

- Amazon advertising campaigns
- Op-Eds to pitch to your local newspapers
- Email newsletters to your email list
- Helpful resources for your website
- Bonus chapters or illustrations for your book
- Keynote speeches you might give
- Writing groups you might lead

Do you see what I mean here? This type of content can be scheduled, too, maybe not in some sort of scheduling app, but in terms of the time you devote to it. Maybe you devote every Sunday morning to updating your Amazon ads. Or every other Sunday. Or the first Sunday of the month. Or every other month. Maybe you plot out event topics for once a month. Or once a quarter. Or once a year. **Whatever works for you.** You just need to be consistent and realistic. Plan to engage with your audience in a way that feels fun and sustainable for you. That's an Evergreen Author.

Likes, Comments, Etc.

When I worked as a marketing director at Wise Ink, I often joked that my title should have been "Author Therapist." That was because navigating these delicate social media and platform-building waters makes authors very, very vulnerable.

*No one is liking my posts. I put my heart and soul into
  this platform and I can't even get one or two likes?
I keep encouraging people to share my book and my
  message, but no one does. I'm humiliated.
I feel like I'm wasting my time here. I chose Twitter
  because I know how active my readers are there, but
  that space is so saturated with authors that I feel like
  I'm screaming into the wind.*

I get it. I completely, totally get it. There's no way for me
to sugar coat this: Discovering the platforms, posts, and strategies that *don't* work can sometimes be painful. I can beg
and plead for you to not worry about likes and comments
until I'm blue in the face, but it's never going to make it so
the disappointment doesn't sting. Here's what you need to
remember before we move on:

1. Building an audience anywhere takes time.
   Give it time. I suggest going "all in" for six
   months before making any decisions around
   whether or not to continue on that specific
   platform.
2. Some people are more active on social media
   than others. Just because you aren't getting a
   ton of comments and likes doesn't mean no
   one is seeing or enjoying what you're putting
   out there. Please, please, please do not equate
   your self-worth with a "like" button.

"An Evergreen Author owns exactly who they are and what gave them the confidence to write a book in the first place."

Most importantly, you're going to learn in step 7 of the Evergreen Author Process that you need to become a data analyst. We'll talk about that in much more detail, but I'll leave it at this: **Do not let your emotions determine what is working and what isn't working.** The data will tell you what's resonating, and that won't always be measured by likes and comments.

Create a platform that you love to continue building upon, and the rest will follow.

Chapter 4 Recap:

- Your platform is a combination of who you are and who you can reach. Use the Pareto Principle to zero in on connecting with your ideal audience.
- Engage in platforms with intention. This means scheduling posts, being thoughtful with your content as well as your time and energy, and above all, finding ways to connect with your readers that bring you joy.

CHAPTER 5

Launch with Intention

If you've already launched a book and are tempted to skip this chapter because you think it doesn't apply to you, bear with me, okay?

I have some really important things to say about book launches, things that are likely going to contradict everything you've heard about launching your book. And this is going to especially apply to an author who wants an Evergreen Author career.

I firmly believe that the conventional wisdom around book launches applies to the one-and-done author—the author who has written one book and doesn't have another book in them.

I also think that the conventional wisdom around book launches applies exclusively to rich extroverts.

Gasp!

I've written four books (well, five if you include this one). For my first book, I was highly encouraged to have a big book launch, so I did. I spent a lot of time, money, and energy creating a great event. But it wasn't me. I sold a ton of books and hosted a great party at an amazing bookstore, but I genuinely hate being the center of attention, especially if it's due to a book I've written. I was so uncomfortable. There was no joy in that marketing experience for me.

For my second book, I refused to repeat that same mistake, so I did nothing. I didn't even post on social media to let people know I had another book out. This was also an enormous mistake. How would the people who liked my first book know that there was another one out there? Answer: they wouldn't. My book sat and sat for a while.

So what gives? How do I launch a book in a way that will work for me? More importantly, how can YOU launch a book in a way that will work for you?

I've found that the answer is simpler than we realize. It starts by leaving any preconceived notions about what a book launch should look like at the door. There is no "right" way to launch (or re-launch) a book.

When you do what's fun and organic to YOU, your book, your brand, and your message, then you're doing it right. When you do this and combine it with a clear budget and reasonable expectations, you're starting a truly Evergreen Author career.

The Conventional Book Launch

It might sound like I'm dumping on the conventional book launch process, but that's really not so. I have been to book launches that were absolutely amazing. Some of these were as well produced and beautiful as a wedding reception, while others were as simple and easy as cupcakes in an author's backyard.

Conventional book launches are a fabulous way of gathering your friends, family, and local community—people who love and support you and will buy your book no matter what—together to share in your success.

If throwing a party around the launch of your book sounds fun for you, DO IT! Make your event for your book the celebration you've always wanted. And invite me, please! I'd love to come.

Looking for some ideas? I've got more than a few:

- Cookbook author? Host a cooking demo and invite all your friends and family.
- Fiction author? Host a cosplay event where people dress up like the characters in your story.
- Nonfiction author? Host an event with guest speakers in your field.
- Children's book author? Take over the gym at your local community center on a Saturday morning and host a story time.
- Poet? Host a reading at a local coffeeshop.
- Photographer? Host an event that includes a photobooth.

For any of these events you could:

- Hire a DJ, balloon artist, or bartender.
- Do a reading from your book.
- Host a guest speaker.
- Collect emails to add to your email list.
- Partner with a local caterer.
- Create a sale on bulk orders of your book.

I have been to book launch events that included professional actors, dancers, and models. I've been to launch event fashion shows, virtual-reality simulations, hands-on demonstrations, and art tables. I've had tons of fun food and drinks. In other words, the sky's the limit. So if this sounds fun and awesome to you, get planning!

For much, much more on how to host an epic book launch, check out our course at Evergreen Authors called Book Launch Blueprint. We have a bonus section of that course dedicated to all the logistics of how to throw a profitable book launch.

So I Don't Need to Throw a Book Launch if I Don't Want To?

No, you don't. Remember what I said at the beginning: An Evergreen Author doesn't do anything for the marketing process that fills them with dread.

However . . . you absolutely must do SOMETHING to "launch" your book.

"You can launch your book in a way that is fun and organic to you."

I've already told you I've done this both ways—the huge party launch way and the do-nothing launch way, neither of which were right for me.

By the time my third book came out, I had the benefit of hindsight. I knew that I had to do *something* to launch my book, but what? After I figured out how much money I was willing to spend on my book launch (somewhere around $200), I spent some time reflecting on what I'd learned; what I liked doing and what I didn't like doing; and strategies that I thought I could try. These were strategies that I'd seen other authors do that sounded okay to me and that were going to fall within my very small budget.

Here's what I came up with:

- Make a list of 25 educational institutions who might be interested in bulk orders of my book. Send them a complimentary copy of my book and a handwritten note. (Cost: $50)
- Create a long-form blog post announcing my new book and posting on Facebook and Pinterest. Promote those posts in August, when teachers are doing their prep work for the new school year. (Cost: $25 in ad spend per platform, totaling $50)
- Reach out to local schools to see if they'd be interested in promoting my book or hosting me for an event. (Free)
- Send out an email to my email list. (Free)

- Hop on the educational Twitter chats I'm part
  of and let people know I have 10 copies of my
  new book to give away. (Cost: $25 in shipping)
- Save any additional budget (~$75) for an Amazon ad campaign for the month of August.

That's it. No parties. No food. This sounded doable and worked really well *for me*.

You might think that this sounds like a really barebones launch strategy—it is! But I've seen book launches with even smaller budgets work equally well. In fact, I've seen authors absolutely kill it by doing *just one thing* that makes sense for them:

- Maybe they focus solely on getting themselves booked on podcasts (this is free, and only costs you your time!).
- Maybe they spend each and every cent on an ad campaign on one great platform, such as Amazon.
- Maybe they focus on a mail marketing campaign to strategic influencers.

The point is that no matter what your budget is, **you can launch your book in a way that is fun and organic to you AS WELL AS within your means.** If you want a party, throw a party. If you don't, don't. If you want to do one thing, do one thing well. If you want to do multiple things, do them all!

We talk a lot at Evergreen Authors about how this is such a great time to be a writer, and this is why. Gone are the days when you had to publish your book on a certain day of the week, in a certain season. You don't need to rely on your local paper to review your book to make it known, and you don't need to be hosted by a bookstore in order to get your book seen by your ideal readers. You can make the launch look exactly the way you want it to look.

Choose wisely and have fun with it!

Cautionary Tales

Generally speaking, when authors have been really thoughtful, realistic, and intentional when their book launches, everything falls into place for their Evergreen Author career when their book comes out, and quickly. That's because they've put their efforts toward the things that bring them joy, aren't caught up in what other authors are doing, and generally have a good attitude that this whole book marketing game is something they can't take too seriously.

I worked with an author once who said it best: "Creating my book has been the highlight of my adult life. If I can make a difference in at least one person's life because of it, I'll know it was all worth it."

When I see authors in this headspace, I am so relieved. Whether you're indie or traditionally published, or working on a huge budget or none at all, going into this process with your head on straight is the key to longevity. As you can imagine, however, this is easier said than done.

We're talking about creative work here. In some cases, we're talking about people's life stories and legacy. Easy for me to advise not taking it too seriously, right?

I hear that and I agree. I'm one of you, remember? I've been riding the ups and downs of the writer's life since I started penning my own stories in the second grade. If writing, publishing, and marketing a book were easy, everyone would do it.

The key mistake for authors when launching their books is getting in their own way. What do I mean by that? Well, for each author it's different, but it boils down to letting our fears and insecurities guide our decisions, instead of our logic and reason.

Here are eight things I see authors do wrong when launching their books:

1. **They hire a publicist, thinking that a publicist can make them famous.** This is number 1 for a reason. Don't think I'm hating on publicists here—I'm not. For authors with huge budgets and wide market appeal, a publicist might make sense. But for the average author, spending $1000–$3000 per month to have someone send (largely unanswered) emails on their behalf is a huge waste of money and effort. You absolutely do not need a publicist to make your book and brand known.

2. **They blow through their budget on silly things.** I have fallen victim to this, and it goes back to those insecurities that creep up any time you're doing something new and exciting and scary. An Evergreen Author is very careful with their budget and doesn't get caught up in something shiny just because it's there. Yes, a caricature artist would be amazing at the launch for your children's book. No, you don't need to have one if it's not in your budget.

3. **They don't make it personal.** Unless you're already a famous celebrity, chances are that the vast majority of people who show up at your launch event, whatever that looks like, are your friends and family. Reach out to people personally. Thank them for coming and sharing your book with others. Acknowledge that you can't do this without them! I'm always amazed at the number of authors who forget to recognize the people around them who have shared in their dream and believed in them. When authors show appreciation, they're also encouraging their supporters to share the book with their networks, too. A little appreciation goes a very long way.

4. **They don't speak at their event.** This absolutely slays me! If you're hosting a launch event where people are coming to see you, you need to speak! People are expecting you

to share your book and your experience with
them. Read from your book! Share a couple
of fun stories about your publishing journey!
This is a book event—share your book!

5. **They don't optimize sales.** Chances are, your
launch event will be one of your biggest days
for sales EVER. Again, the people who show
up to your launch events are people who are
going to support you—let them support you!
Don't discount your book on launch day.
Don't give away copies to people who will
buy your book no matter what! (We talk a
lot about this in our Book Launch Blueprint
course-—being financially smart is crucial at
launch time!)

6. **They are falsely modest.** I've brought this up
more than once now, so hopefully you've gotten it through your head that this is not a good
strategy to sell books. Do not—and I repeat—
do NOT go on social media to announce your
book, then minimize your experience or work
in any way. I often see authors do this by saying things like, "I just published on Amazon,"
or "It's not like I have an agent or anything."
99.9 percent of people couldn't care less HOW
you published your book. They just want to
know that it's a good read! Why should anyone get excited for your book if YOU aren't
excited for it?

7. **They don't take great photos.** If you're holding an in-person event, you need someone (not you) to take pictures. This doesn't have to be a professional photographer, but it does need to be someone who will get lots of photos that you can use for content in the months and years to come. Again, we talk about this a lot in our Book Launch Blueprint course.

8. **They think small.** Yes, your launch is about your book and your brand. But as we will discover in the next section, an Evergreen Author finds lasting success through **partnerships.** You've already started some of that work by connecting with other authors and small business owners who are doing things right. So if you're hosting an event, it's the time to reach out to those people and ask for a social media post or share, or maybe invite them to speak at your event. Opening your event OUT to the wider community means you'll be tapping into their networks, too.

Think about it this way: Your launch, whatever it looks like, is going to set the stage for your writing career. Be open and flexible with how you launch your book and you'll be amazed at all the opportunities you have.

"You'll be constantly launching and re-launching your book each time you take bold steps to put it out into the world."

What if My Book Launched a Long Time Ago?

Remember how I told you to bear with me if your book has already launched? Well, you made it: This section is for you.

The single best thing about being an indie author is that you control all aspects of the experience. That includes your production, your format, your launch, EVERYTHING. It also includes your launch strategy.

Did you have any pangs of regret that you didn't host an awesome launch event when your book first came out? **How about a re-launch?**

Did you think any of the ideas I threw out about mail marketing, readings, or party ideas sounded like something you'd love to do? **Do them now!**

I once worked with an author who had launched her book really prematurely. She'd rushed through editing, gotten a cover she didn't love, and hosted a really small gathering to celebrate her book, all because she felt like she needed to have her book done by a certain date.

But she was filled with regrets. Every time she picked up her book, she was reminded of how she didn't launch it the way she wanted. Specifically, she really wanted a new cover. And while she was at it, she wanted to make some corrections and changes to the text.

Of course this isn't an ideal situation, but being an Evergreen Author means making lemonade out of lemons sometimes. As her book cover was being redesigned and she worked through some edits in the text, I encouraged her to reach out to one of her mentors to write a foreword for the book. Now, her new cover would not only look better, but it would also include an indicator that it was a revised second edition, as well as several new endorsements.

In publishing terms, a revised second edition is a new book. New ISBN, new look, new content. This means: **a new chance to launch.**

This time, her event was exactly what she wanted it to be. She held her "re-launch" at a bookstore she loved, invited everyone she'd missed the first time, and had her son play live music, something she knew the crowd would love (they did!).

Maybe your book doesn't need a re-do. Maybe you're considering an audiobook version—how about creating a launch strategy around that?

Maybe you aren't creating anything new, but you host a birthday party for your book? (This is a great option for authors who just can't turn down the opportunity to host a party!)

Maybe you're just super inspired by the idea of getting in front of people in a new way, so you throw an event like a reading, or a book club, or a demonstration, or some sort of partnership, and **you do it because it's a way to connect to your audience and add value to your community?**

This is why we added this step in the Evergreen Author process to this book. Your book launches once, that's true, but you'll be constantly launching and re-launching your book each time you take bold steps to put it out into the world.

When I figured out the launch strategy that worked for me, it was liberating. I know that no matter how many books

I have left in me, I have ways of getting that book out there that feel right and are effective. I don't have to break the bank, I don't have to host any parties (yay!), and I don't have to sell my soul or do anything that feels awkward or uncomfortable for me. Neither do you!

Chapter 5 Recap:

- Your launch event can look any way you want it to look. Choose a plan that works for you and your budget.
- Your launch event isn't a once-in-a-lifetime opportunity. As long as you're an Evergreen Author, you should be thinking of new ways to launch and relaunch your book, in ways that feel right for you.

CHAPTER 6

Partnerships and Ad Strategy

I know it's not nice to play favorites, but this is my favorite chapter of this book. That's because by the time you've really let it sink in that this whole book marketing process can look any way you want it to look, the work we'll talk about in this chapter becomes really fun and fulfilling.

I'm going to start with a story from a business book author I worked with several years ago. He's one of those jet-setting, always-on-the-go kind of entrepreneurs. He'd worked in several Fortune 500 companies and was constantly surrounded by thought leaders in his field, many of whom had written books and carried somewhat famous last names. His book was a step-by-step finance guide for young entrepreneurs. It was filled with swear words and irreverent humor.

Steps 1–5 of his Evergreen Author plan were completed with ease. This guy knew exactly who he was and how he wanted to reach people. He didn't have any dreams of winding up on Oprah's book club list. He had absolutely no interest in social media or a huge launch event. He was laser focused on his ultimate goal—using his book to build his business.

He made a list of five major players in the finance world. These were people he had connections with already, but not close ones. He knew that he had one shot to get it right—if he came off as just another schmuck trying to tap into these people's networks, he was sunk. Knowing that if he sent an email directly to one of these finance people that it would probably never get read, he spent some time figuring out who their *assistants* were. He figured out how to get in touch with them, what their pain points might be in the organization, and how he could be helpful.

In his emails to the assistants, he introduced himself and made his connection to their boss known. In one instance, he offered to do a free, one-hour training session for the team. In another instance, he offered to send a complimentary copy of the book to them, along with a discount code for a bulk order. In another instance, he asked to be connected to their events coordinator to see if he could do a lunchtime book signing event in the office.

This strategy worked like a charm. After his initial pitch, he proved himself and his worth to the companies he reached out to and was booked as a consultant at each organization. **He tailored his work to each company and included copies of his book with each training session he led.**

He sold out of his first print run (over 5000 copies!) within the first six months. There was no launch event. No social media. He did it just by creating lasting partnerships.

Partnerships, 101

In life, partnerships are everything. Absolutely everything. But for some reason, authors don't see this when they first embark on the marketing work for their books. It might be because selling books can seem, on the surface, to be purely transactional. *I have a product, you buy the product, see you later!*

That might be true for your next takeout lunch meal, but it's not so when it comes to books. Think about it — purchasing and reading a book is a commitment. You do this when you walk into a bookstore or browse books on Amazon. You're not going to purchase a book if you're not willing to spend time sitting with it and reading through its pages.

It doesn't matter if you have a nonfiction or a fiction book, indie or traditionally published. **Your book is one of thousands and thousands published each and every day.** There are ways to get your book noticed that are based on keywords and algorithms, which we will talk about in the next section, but for an Evergreen Author, it's the partnerships you make that will create a lasting career.

Okay, fine. I see how a small business owner who writes nonfiction would want to focus on a partnership strategy. But I'm just a nobody writing fiction. I can't make partnerships like this.

You're right, you can't make partnerships like *that*. But you *can* make partnerships.

One of the most effective partnership strategies for fiction authors involves creating value for their local community. I've seen authors do workshops on the writing or illustration process at their local community center, or forming a writers group. I've seen children's book authors take over story times, self-help writers lead retreats at retreat centers, and authors (myself included!) work directly with school districts, becoming adjunct teachers and consultants.

The point is that the opportunities are out there, but you need to get creative in seeking them out. They are more than likely not going to just fall in your lap. I repeat:

> **Partnership opportunities are out there, no matter what you write. The difference between an author and an Evergreen Author is that the Evergreen Author doesn't wait for life to happen to them. They go out and make life happen.**

Win-Win Partnerships

Have I convinced you yet that this whole book marketing experience is whatever you make it? I hope so. Because this is where it gets really, really good.

By this point you understand that the creation of your book and the creation of your platform are entirely up to you. You should be working with a book concept and/or finished product that you can stand by.

Now you get to take all that research you did looking into other authors, all those relationships you've created on your chosen platforms, and all the ways in which you've committed to reaching people consistently and sustainably, and start pitching yourself as a partner to people and entities that might benefit from your expertise.

Now, when authors get to this point, their insecurities tend to take over.

What expertise? I don't have any expertise!

Sure you do. You wrote a book, didn't you? Stop undervaluing your work already! What value do you bring to your readers? Entertainment? A specific knowledge base? **Focus on how you can add specific and tangible value for your readers.**

I worked with a cookbook author once who didn't question that she was a great chef, but felt that as a self-taught cook, she couldn't add much value to the culinary schools and accounts she followed on Instagram. She was anxious to make partnerships, but she didn't know how.

She thought long and hard about what her true talents were in the kitchen. When she did that, she realized that while her food was good, she really shined when she was cooking for large groups of families, particularly families who were trying to eat healthy while traveling for sports.

After putting together a thoughtful pitch, she partnered with her local community center to create a monthly cooking class where she created meal plans and helped families prep food for a month of travel.

Here's why this is a win-win. First off, she was providing specific value to her community. Her pitch to the community center didn't come from a place trying to sell books—it was about **providing value** (more on this in the next section).

The next, and probably equally important, reason this was such a brilliant marketing strategy was purely financial. This author's book was listed at $24.99. Depending on how she sold the books (direct or through a wholesaler), she made approximately $10 per book sale. In an average month, she was making around $200 in book sales. Not bad, but she was hardly going to be retiring on that income.

When she taught her monthly meal prep course, she made $200 **per person.** The community center kitchen held 10 chefs, so she was pulling in $2000/month with that event, minus the cost of food.

It gets better. Once word spread about her meal prep classes, she was asked to do in-home cooking demos and meal prep workshops. She kept her slot at the community center, but also added on a bonus day for holiday meal prep, and then another evening for meal prep for kids.

That's an Evergreen Author. The book is secondary to the experience she provides. She's made a career doing what she loves.

I've seen this type of partnership work out for fiction and nonfiction authors alike. I've seen authors make serious money offering writing workshops and retreats, leading in-home brainstorming or creative sessions, being a keynote speaker at major companies or events, and being a frequent guest on talk shows and podcasts.

All it takes is a little reflection, intentional planning, and a win-win partnership.

The Win-Lose Partnership

I keep talking about how it really bugs me when authors let their creative insecurities take over when it comes to creating partnerships. I hope you've gotten it through your heads by now that you're not going to sell any books by leading with fear.

Well, on the flip side of that, there are authors who get to this stage of the Evergreen Author process and are, shall we say, a little less than humble. Those authors know exactly what value they bring to the table, and they're ready to shout it from the rooftops.

There's no one who adds value like I add value! Here's a list of organizations that would be lucky to have me around! And now that I have a book out, I'll be doubling my speaking fee! Cha-ching!

In some ways, I love this confidence. These authors are brave and energetic, therefore bound to succeed, right?

Well, here's the thing. When authors focus solely on what they bring to the table, and not **what the potential partner might need them to bring to the table**, their chances of creating a real, lasting partnership are much slimmer.

For example, I worked with an author a while back who was a bit of a local celebrity. With his platforms, he had no doubt that his book was going to be instantly successful. He wasn't wrong. Just one Facebook post with information to preorder his book went gangbusters. Lucky guy!

The problem began when he started doing his outreach to larger organizations. Now that he had a book, he was ready to start pitching himself to national conferences. This was a great strategy for him! Unfortunately, his pitches were blast emails and looked something like this:

> *Dear Sir or Madam,*
>   *I would like to be included in your guest speaker lineup for your upcoming event. Here is my website. My speaking fee is attached. Looking forward to hearing from you.*

He was met with crickets across the board with this strategy, and not just because the pitch itself was bland and impersonal (though that didn't help). **He was missing the part where he said why anyone should consider him in the first place.**

It took this author a while to figure out what he was doing wrong here. He was presenting himself as a branded celebrity, which was off-putting and arrogant. Within his local circles, this might work, but he made a huge mistake assuming this would work beyond his local network.

In contrast, my business partner, Josie, wrote a self-help book about gratitude. Josie was a school counselor and didn't exactly have celebrity status — she just had a book that she believed in and knew would resonate with people.

Her pitches took a lot more time to curate. She included a personal salutation, the story behind her book, and the ideas she had about working together. She did her research about any upcoming events she wanted to be a part of and what specific things she could do to draw more attendance.

She promised to use her platforms to promote the event herself.

She found this strategy so effective for speaking events and signings that she ended up quitting her day job to focus on speaking.

An Evergreen Author understands something very fundamental about partnerships: **they are a two-way street.** Bookstores are in the business of making money, so **pitch a partnership with them that assures they will make money.** Event hosts are in the business of keeping their audiences engaged and happy, so pitch a partnership with them that assures their audiences will be engaged and happy.

If this sounds good to you, but you worry that you need to hire some sort of expensive publicist to do this work, *you don't*. It's time consuming to be sure, and if it's totally out of the realm of possibility for you to do this type of pitching, you have options to hire a virtual assistant or intern.

You do not need to spend thousands on a publicist. You don't!

This is so important to us at Evergreen Authors that we put together a downloadable "Little Black Book" of marketing templates that real-life authors have used to pitch themselves for mutually beneficial partnerships. Head over to our website to check it out!

Out-of-the-Box Partnership Ideas

Back in the day, authors had very limited ways to partner with people or entities to get themselves out there. Typically, authors did bookstore readings, coffeeshop readings, and might get lucky with a few bulk orders for events.

Nowadays, thanks to social media and a shift in how we think about supporting local businesses, there are TONS of options for authors to make really lasting partnerships. Here are a few ideas I've seen work wonders. Keep in mind that this is not a checklist. These situations won't work for all books. You know your book and your audience best. Let adding value and establishing a real, win-win personal connection be your guide!

- Subscription boxes—Can you pitch your book to be included in a subscription box?
- Free gift with purchase—Can you partner with a gift shop to include your gift with purchase?
- Social media influencers—Can you ask a social media influencer to review your book on their platform?
- Buy one, get one offers—Can you create a BOGO offer on your website for the holidays?
- Bulk orders for events or libraries—Can you pitch your book for a specific cause or event?
- Class sets—Can you pitch your book to a school or as training material?

When authors get to this point and start getting really excited about putting themselves and their work out there in unique ways, I inevitably am asked the same question:

Reaching out personally to people, organizations, event coordinators, administrators . . . all of this is taking so much time. Isn't there an easier way to do this?

You have now reached the pivotal moment in the Evergreen Author process where you must realize the truth:

People can spot a phony, scamming, or disingenuous person from a mile away.

Partnerships are *relationships*, and you're not going to create a trusting relationship with a blast email to every subscription box company in your state.

If time is the issue, hire a virtual assistant or intern to do this outreach for you. We have examples of how authors have done this really effectively in our "Little Black Book of Marketing Templates" available on our website.

But no, the bottom line is that there is no "easy" way to do this work. It takes time, thought, and patience.

I cannot tell you how much I believe in partnerships. I have seen authors create event series, curricula, and enormous bulk order sales opportunities just because they were thoughtful about how they approached people with their partnerships and made it a win-win situation for both parties. **Any work you do involving partnerships, even ones**

that don't work out, will ultimately be extremely beneficial to you as you learn what audiences and readers really want.

But again, if creating partnerships to sell your book is filling you with dread, skip it. You can always come back to this at any point in your author journey.

In the meantime, you're going to want to enter into a different kind of partnership, one I believe each and every author should use: a workable advertising strategy.

Yuck, advertising?

Stay with me here, people. This is really, really important. I was a published author for more than five years before I took out one ad on my books. Five. Years.

Keep this in mind: I wasn't exactly twiddling my thumbs during those five years. I was hustling to create partnerships. I was speaking at schools, doing book clubs, and coordinating bulk orders of my books to youth groups.

I was working my tail off. Don't get me wrong—I loved it. But I wasn't great about managing my time.I spent weekends away at educational conferences and long hours in the car driving from school to school doing author visits. With two very young children, I burned out pretty quickly. I didn't know how long this author hustle was sustainable for me.

I knew that advertising was something people did, but I felt weird about it. In my mind, advertising meant one of two yucky things:

1. Spending a ton of money
2. Cheesy ad copy that no one reads anyway

"**Partnership opportunities are out there. Get creative and seek them out!**"

I admit that I'm showing my age here. The idea of advertising my book online, on the platforms I'd chosen, just didn't really occur to me. I was imagining taking out an ad in the newspaper or something like that. Maybe it's a Gen X thing.

Regardless, it was then that I met Josie, my partner in crime. She was selling more books than I was and she was working far less. Her secret was simple: she was advertising on Amazon.

The Pareto Principle, Again

Remember how we talked in a previous chapter about the 80/20 rule? The one that says 20 percent of your efforts will lead to 80 percent of your sales?

Well, forgive me, because I'm going to geek out a little bit about how this applies to advertising on your chosen platforms.

Let's say you're on Facebook and you're blogging. You have everything automated, and you're enjoying the process. Your book is available on Amazon and Indie Bound, as well as directly from your website. You're doing all the right things. All is well.

That's awesome, but I have some hard truth for you to swallow: These platforms you've chosen are SATURATED with authors just like you. They, too, are posting awesome content on Facebook. They, too, have their book available in multiple formats on Amazon. They, too, are doing all the right things.

It's an amazing time to be an author because you have so many free tools at your disposal to create an awesome platform.

Oops, did I say free? Because these platforms you're on (and I include Amazon as a platform here) — they're not free.

I mean, it's free *entry*, I suppose. But there's a reason that the founders of Facebook and Amazon and all these other "free" platforms are among the richest people in the world.

You guessed it — advertising.

If you want your book to stand out on any of these given platforms, you're going to have to advertise there.

When I say this to authors, they tend to get a little panicky. *Wait a second. I'm active on several different platforms. How do I know where to advertise? And how much? And what about the technology? I don't know how to do this!*

I understand that feeling completely, and it's the same feeling I had at first. But when you go back to the Pareto Principle, it becomes a bit simpler. Understand that you want to focus on that 20 percent of your efforts that are leading to sales and get really laser focused there. Ask yourself:

Where does my audience buy books?

Advertise your book there.

On what platform am I hoping to grow my author business?

Advertise your book there.

That's it. It's that simple. Don't worry about what other authors are doing, and don't get caught up with whatever the latest, greatest advertising trends are.

Advertise your book in places where your ideal readers are searching for it.

Let's Talk About Amazon

Full disclosure: I'm a big yoga hippie and have many problems with Amazon. As a general rule, I don't buy things there. I have hope that they will improve their hiring practices, work conditions, and impact on the environment, but as of now, Amazon has some work to do. I also am fully aware that Amazon is killing indie bookstores and small business in general.

Here's what I need you all to understand:

Like it or not, Amazon is the biggest bookseller in the world. By a wide, wide margin. Any author would be crazy not to have their book on that platform.

Here's what I also need you all to understand:

Because of the ubiquity of Amazon and the ease of the customer experience

**there, people are buying more books
and reading more than ever.**

It's true. Let it sink in. People are reading more books now than ever before.

Amazon has made the publishing dream come true for countless people. It has made it so you don't need to be a celebrity or have a traditional agent or publisher to get your work out into the world. And while yes, people might not be patronizing their local bookstores as much anymore, I'm seeing that pendulum swing as smart bookstore owners get creative about getting people through the doors. They're hosting more events, opening restaurants in the stores, and getting really creative about how they showcase authors. (See why I get really excited about partnerships?)

Amazon isn't going anywhere, not for the foreseeable future. And because it's the biggest platform in the world for people buying books, and you're one of thousands and thousands of authors on that platform, you're going to have to put some ad dollars behind your book to get it noticed. People are hungrier than ever for what you're selling. Like it or not, they're going to Amazon to figure out what book to download or listen to next.

So yes, you're welcome to have your feelings about publishing and selling books on Amazon. Yes, Amazon is going to take a piece of your book sales. Yes, Amazon is a thorn in the side of small businesses with their deep discounts and two-hour shipping options. Yes, Amazon has work to do to be a better global corporation. But Amazon *has also* created a really, really easy platform for you to reach people who are searching for books like yours, which we will talk about in the next section.

The Search Engine

The thing that changed the game for me was understanding something pretty simple about Amazon (and Pinterest, while we're at it): These websites are search engines in the same way that Google is a search engine.

If you just read that sentence and rolled your eyes because you already knew this, I guess you can skip to the next section. But for me, this was like a major lightbulb over the head moment. Think about it. When you go to look for something you need online, what do you do? You Google it. Google is the world's biggest search engine.

But when you're looking for something specific you want to buy, what do you do? Chances are, you'll go to Amazon to see if they sell it. You might not ultimately buy it from there. You might go there just to see reviews about the product. You might consider competitive products. You might find yourself drawn to the "also bought" section to see what else is out there that's similar to what you're looking for. This is how people are using Amazon.

More specifically, this is how people are using Amazon to find their next book.

People who love historical fiction set during the Renaissance are going to search *using that phrase* on Amazon: "Historical Fiction Renaissance."

People looking for a book to teach them how to build their own treehouse are going to search using *that* phrase: "How To Build a Treehouse Book."

People looking for a cozy mystery gift set are going to search using that phrase: "Cozy Mystery Book Gift Set."

People who can't get enough memoirs written by professional athletes will *continually* search Amazon using that type of phrasing: "Tennis memoir." "Baseball Memoir." "Kristy Yamaguchi Book."

You want to make it so when people are searching for what they want to read, your book comes up for them, using Amazon's ad platform.

So obvious, right? Why did it take me so long to figure this out? It's another one of life's mysteries. But I haven't told you the best part yet. Once I figured out how to use Amazon (and Pinterest) as the search engines they are, it meant that **I was only advertising to people who wanted my book.** No more awkward Facebook posts begging random people to buy my book.

No more guessing about whether or not people were seeing my ads at all. (Much more on this in the next chapter.)

When I realized I could use Amazon in this way, it was

totally freeing. As much as I loved the partnerships I'd made, **knowing that I could get consistent sales simply by activating some keywords and phrases was liberating.**

It meant that I could keep writing. I didn't have to hustle so hard. I was selling my book to people who were already searching for it. Game changer.

Now for some Q + A

What is this going to cost me?

When we talk about Amazon advertising at Evergreen Authors, we find people are worried we're trying to sell them on a huge investment. Sometimes they've already spent thousands on a print ad that got them nowhere. Sometimes they're just simply done with all the screaming into the wind they've been doing.

Are you ready for this? We suggest authors start running ads at $3 per day. In order to get some good data (which we'll talk much more about in the next chapter), you'll want to run those ads consistently for about three months.

Let's see, $3 per day, times 120 days is . . . $360.

That's what you spend. We're hoping that once you figure out how to do this, you'll be making far more than that in book sales.

Obviously, the more you spend, the more you have the potential to earn. The amount you spend is proportional to how many people you reach. There are plenty of people out there spending THOUSANDS on ads on multiple platforms.

If that's in your budget, go right ahead. But for the average Evergreen Author, the cost of a cup of coffee per day is manageable and sustainable for the long haul, especially at the beginning.

I'm not technical. Can't I pay someone to do this for me?

Sure. You can pay anyone to do anything for you nowadays. But here's what we say at Evergreen Authors: **If I can learn how to run Amazon ads, so can you.** I promise you, I am maybe the least technical person in the universe. And I did it! Plus, we created a really simple online course called Algorithm Alchemy to teach you how to do it yourself. Once you know how to do it yourself, you can do it for the *lifetime of your writing career*. Not just for one book, but for any book that you write until the end of time.

That said, you absolutely can pay someone to take over your ads for you. Just be prepared to pay handsomely (I'm talking hundreds of dollars or more, on top of what you'd spend on the ads themselves) for that service.

Ad Strategy

Ad strategy sounds like complicated marketing speak but it's really, really simple.

It just means being intentional about where, how, and how much you spend on advertising.

By this point, you should have already established a platform that seems manageable to you, and hopefully you have that automated so whether you're posting and interacting with people three times per day or three times per year, you have a plan.

Now all you have to do is make a plan to advertise on your chosen platforms.

Here's an example I think most authors can wrap their heads around as they start. I worked with an author/blogger who was really active on Facebook and Pinterest but working on a small ad budget. Her book wasn't coming out for another year, so she didn't have anything to promote yet. She just wanted to build her audience.

Her plan looked like this:

1. Boost my "Monthly Roundup" post on Facebook, first Friday of the month (Cost: $25 max)
2. Create a "Holiday Freebie" ad to run on Facebook October–November (Cost: $50 max over eight weeks)
3. Promote my "Best of" Pinterest post in December (Cost: $10 max)

To be clear, she is spending $85 *for the entire year* on advertising. She easily could have added a couple more zeros after any of those numbers and reached more people, since the more you spend the more people you reach, but for the time being that was all she could comfortably budget.

Similarly, we've worked with plenty of authors over the years who skip advertising on any of their platforms because they know Amazon is where it's at for them. Their ad strategy might look something like this:

1. Spring: $100/month
2. Summer: $50/month
3. Fall: $200/month
4. Winter: $0

Why wouldn't an author just spend the same amount every month on Amazon? Well, sales ebb and flow, as we'll discuss in the next chapter. If you aren't sure what your sales cycle will look like, don't sweat it. Just start with whatever you can for three months, and then go from there.

The example I just gave would have been from an author who understood she didn't usually see a lot of activity in winter or summer, so she focused her efforts on spring and fall.

For my books, I go full force in the summer, since that's when I know teachers are buying books for the classroom. My business partner Josie's book on gratitude sells like hotcakes in November, so she goes full force on ads that month.

It's simply a matter of paying attention to your sales and giving your ads time to run to give you data you can use moving forward.

Do you see how this is an Evergreen effort? I cannot begin to tell you how many authors I've seen become totally liberated by this knowledge of how to make automation and ad strategy work for them. No more trying things just to see if they'll work and no more trying to sell your book to people who don't want it.

Ad strategy means taking these "free" platforms and making sure that the people who are already searching for your content find it easily. That's it. It really is that simple.

Chapter 6 Recap:

- Focus on real, personal, win-win partnerships. These don't happen overnight. Be thoughtful and intentional with all your outreach efforts.
- If you want people to see your book and content, you must advertise on the platforms you've chosen. It's not hard, and it's not expensive. Do yourself a favor and learn how to do it so you can take that knowledge with you your entire writing career.

CHAPTER 7

Become a Scientist

As my high school physics teacher would be happy to attest, I'm no scientist. So no, you're not going to be mixing chemicals in this last step in the Evergreen Author process.

What you WILL be doing is something even more important: You're going to take all the thoughtful efforts you've already made — creating a beautiful book, a workable platform, and a sustainable ad strategy — and bring those together to create a mosaic for you to study and learn from.

In other words, you're going to step back and look at what the data is telling you. Then you're going to make decisions going forward **based on that data**. Sounds easy, right?

Not so fast.

The Unemotional Writer

I'm going to let you in on the key difference between an author and an Evergreen Author.

It's not genre. It's not budget. It's not the quality of the book itself.

It's the ability to be *unemotional* about the writing and selling process. This is not easy. I repeat: **This. Is. Not. Easy.**

I'm one of you, remember? These books we create are labors of love. They often include pieces of our selves no one has seen before. Putting your work out there is scary and intensely vulnerable, especially if you've written a story about your own life or the work you've dedicated your life to.

I've seen one bad review reduce an author to tears. I've seen several authors who build their reputations around their tough exteriors break down completely when they realize their book isn't selling the way they'd hoped. I've seen some of the most talented writers I've ever come across ask over and over again, *Are you sure this is good? Like really good? You're not just saying that, are you?*

I get it. I get it so much. You have no idea how much **I get this.** I speak from personal experience when I say that while being emotionally attached to your work is absolutely normal, **the most important thing we can do as authors is to detach as much as possible from allowing those emotions to guide our marketing decisions.** This is hard work and will last the lifetime of your creative career.

And just how does an author get unemotional about their book?

They let the data tell them what is working and what isn't.

They make adjustments based on facts and not feelings.

Let me give you an example. I worked with an author who was an incredibly successful CEO at a tech startup. Her story, vision, and platform were nothing short of legendary in her field. When she wrote a book about her life story and all that had brought her to that point of success, she had every right to feel as though it was going to be a resounding success. It was the type of rags to riches story that inspires movies. She wasn't lacking confidence. She knew she had a huge platform and tons of support. She threw an epic launch event and sold hundreds of books in her first week.

Then the Amazon data came in. She'd only sold 100 books in the first three months. She'd printed over 5,000. She'd been counting on all that up-front support she'd gotten from her launch to catapult her book to success. She was devastated. Worse, she'd created a keynote speech around the process of writing her book that she felt sure was going to resonate with young entrepreneurs. Together with her assistant, she pitched herself to more than 20 conferences, all of which turned her down. Six months after the launch of her book, she was beside herself. Why had she written this book in the first place? What was she thinking, putting herself out in the world this way?

If any of this strikes a chord with you, I would like to reach through these pages and give you a hug. This is a tough situation that the vast majority of authors find themselves in at some point. Sadly, this tough situation can make authors make bad decisions. I've seen it time and again.

Since nothing's working, maybe I'll just take out a print ad in my local paper and cross my fingers that someone sees it.

I'm strapped for cash, but maybe if I put a publicist on retainer on my credit card then I'll see results.

Maybe I should call that guy who sent me a DM a few months ago promising to grow my followers by 10k . . .

Maybe I should just donate the copies of the book I have left. I don't think I'm cut out for this. Being an author sucks.

I can tell you right now I've been in this very situation myself. It's not fun. The only way out of it is to take a step back from the "feelings" part. For this particular author, I knew that while the book was still fairly new, we had enough data (and ways to create data) that we could set her on an Evergreen Author path.

Here's how we did that in an unemotional way:

1. We started an Amazon ad campaign. (Well, when I say "we," I mean her assistant took our Algorithm Alchemy course and learned how to create Amazon ads.) She set her budget for $10/day for 6 months.
2. While those ads were running, I had her assistant call each and every company she'd pitched her keynote to and ask for feedback on the pitch itself.

After a few months, we all met up again. The author was still feeling a little down in the dumps about what she felt

was the lack of success for her book. But now we had some
data to work with going forward.

1. When we looked at her Amazon ad campaign,
    we noticed that she was getting sales. But one
    of her keywords was getting **10 times** the clicks
    of the other one. It was actually a phrase she
    had added in passing, but for some reason
    people were searching that phrase on Amazon,
    finding her book, and clicking through to
    read about it. That one keyword phrase alone
    resulted in the sale of 50 books over 2 months.

2. When we looked at the feedback she'd got-
    ten from her failed attempts at partnerships,
    she learned that many of the companies she'd
    been targeting were looking for someone to
    talk more about implementing strategy and
    not the writing process, which is what she'd
    been pitching.

With that data, we realized we had two very clear
action steps:

1. Put more ad spend behind that one keyword
    phrase that was bringing in so many sales. We
    increased the "pay-per-click" budget from 15
    cents to 3 dollars. **The data showed us that this
    keyword was working for her, so it made sense
    to spend more money to reach more people.**

2. Update the keynote speech to address exactly what the companies were searching for, not what the author felt like giving them.

That's it. That's all we did. And it worked. After another 6 months, she realized that her sales were so good with that one keyword that she increased her pay-per-click budget to $5 per click. That's a lot to spend on a keyword, but she knew it would work because **the data showed her it would.** She was easily selling 300 books per month with this strategy.

The keynote speeches were getting booked. Her books were selling consistently and sustainably. It was all thanks to following the data.

Beyond Troubleshooting

The author I just described was like many authors—she needed to troubleshoot what she was doing wrong and fix the problem. No matter what your platforms are, you can do this, too.

You can do some deep diving into the right keywords to use to advertise your book on Amazon. You can look at the analytics on your website and figure out where the vast majority of your traffic is coming from. You can get super nerdy with Excel spreadsheets and cost-benefit analysis.

However, this isn't always easy. For example, when I did Saturday events to promote my first book, I found that the math didn't always add up. If I sold 50 books and made $500 that day, great! But I was also paying a babysitter $200 for a full day of childcare. Plus, I'd missed a Saturday of playtime with my kids. This is yet another example of how a strategy that works for one author might not work for another.

This is why this seventh step in the Evergreen Author process is so critical and lasts the lifetime of your book. Your circumstances will change. Your budget will change. Your platforms will change. You have to be flexible and attentive to those changes if you want to do this for the long haul.

And the best part is that when you do this—when you act more like a data analyst and less emotionally, you will make decisions that will grow your career based on *fact*. Your level of intention will be so much higher. **You won't feel nervous about launching a new effort or trying a new strategy because you'll have data that supports it will work.**

Here's what I mean by that. One author we worked with at Evergreen Authors was deeply invested in his science-fiction fantasy series. He had absolutely no aspirations of becoming famous. He just wanted to sell his books and create a passive stream of income.

He only did two things to promote his book:

1. He ran Amazon ads, which he was constantly watching and adjusting.
2. He created bonus content for his website in the form of bonus chapters and illustrations.

When this author started out, he was sure that Amazon was where it was at for him. (He was right! All of the time he spent there resulted in steady sales with very little effort.) The bonus content was really something fun he did as a creative outlet.

After spending months creating and posting bonus content and additional chapters without much traction, he decided to post a map that he'd had a local artist create to accompany the book. What did he have to lose? He had no reason to think that the map was going to do anything for him other than give him something new for his website and email list.

It turned out that a lot of people who had read his book loved the map. They downloaded it and shared it across multiple platforms. He even found out that someone had created a pin of the illustration for Pinterest and that pin had gone viral.

The author was stunned. He never anticipated that sort of response! However, he could see a clear spike in book sales on Amazon after he published that illustration. So what did he do with that data?

He did more of what was clearly working.

He partnered with the artist to create more maps and character sketches. His website, which he'd always visualized as being very text-heavy, became a home base of illustrations for his book.

This is what I mean by letting the data guide your marketing decisions.

If you think this seems like a no-brainer, I have bad news. Sometimes authors are so emotionally invested in the dream they've created in their heads that they simply don't listen when the data is being very clear.

They keep doing the same things even when those things aren't working. They keep blogging, even though no one is reading. They keep paying a publicist, because that's what someone told them to do. They keep paying to go to conferences where no one buys their book.

These are the authors who, despite all the talent they have, either burn out, give up, or both.

To be clear: **You will make boneheaded decisions when it comes to marketing.** I certainly have. You'll spend money on things that don't work. You might take out an ad somewhere that you feel totally sure about, only to find out it doesn't sell you a single book. You'll spend a Saturday at a signing or a conference that you had high hopes for, with zero results.

You don't know what you don't know, and even the best-informed authors can spend time and effort on things that just don't pan out. That's life. What is it they say about the best laid plans of mice and men?

As long as you haven't gone into debt (something we'd never advise), think of each and every marketing mistake you made as **more data for you to use in the future, not some sort of indicator of your value as a writer.**

Shake it off and move forward, letting the data be your guide.

Chapter 7 Recap:

- Get unemotional about the writing process. This is hard work.
- Let the data be your guide for all of your marketing decisions. Step back and evaluate what's working and not working for you. Do more of what's working.

BONUS CHAPTER 8

Keep Creating... Maybe

Most of the conventional wisdom around publishing a book is that you should always be working on another book, and another, and another.

I really struggled with including this chapter in *The Evergreen Author*. I mean, in some ways, it's good advice—keep those books coming! People who love your work will always be hungry for more from you. And if you love writing, all the better.

But we work with authors who can honestly say that their one book (maybe it's one they wrote for their business, or maybe it's one they wrote for the heck of it) is all they've got in them. They don't want to keep creating.

Guess what? That's cool. Like I've been repeating over and over in this book, you shouldn't do anything that fills you with dread. You don't need to keep creating if you don't want to. Just keep on fine-tuning your partnership and ad strategy, and you can still call yourself an Evergreen Author.

Here's what I want to say to those of you who might be reading this book and are in that not-so-glamourous space that so many of us authors are in: You're working hard, you're hustling in ways that feel enjoyable to you, and you're selling some books. But no, Oprah isn't calling. No, your book isn't on the *New York Times* Bestseller list. And no, you can't quit your day job. Here's the final piece of tough love I want to give you: None of that matters. None of it.

Should you shoot for the stars? Absolutely. But as far as I can see, if you've created a book you are genuinely proud of, you've already reached ultimate success.

Yes, you should market your book in ways that bring you some financial success, too. But *that* success is secondary to the actual creative work, whatever that looks like for you.

I often end our author platform talks with this: **If you're a creative person and aren't creating, then what are you doing?**

We founded Evergreen Authors because we want to help authors keep creating. Whatever that means for you, however that looks for you, keep connecting and creating. The world needs what you have to give!

ACKNOWLEDGMENTS

I'd like to give a heartfelt thank you to each and every author who has trusted me with their stories and visions over the years. Whether it's been through Wise Ink Creative Publishing or through one of our courses at Evergreen Authors, I have never taken for granted that writing and publishing a book is an act of bravery. I'm truly humbled by this work.

Thank you to Dara Beevas and Amy Quale of Wise Ink Creative Publishing. There are no words to describe how much you both mean to me. You both changed the course of my life and helped make my dreams come true. How could I ever repay such a gift?

Thank you to my business partner and soulmate, Josie Robinson. Evergreen Authors is so much fun. You complete me.

Super special thanks to Paul Nylander of illustrada Design, whose quick redesign of the book interior resolved some formatting issues when we went to press. We at Evergreen Authors are so grateful for his expertise and friendship!

Thank you to my husband, Larry, and my little rascals, Anna and Aaron. You're my absolute favorite humans.

ABOUT THE AUTHOR

ROSEANNE CHENG is a former high school English teacher and the award-winning author of three books: *The Take Back of Lincoln Junior High, Edge the Bare Garden,* and *The Tireless Teacher Toolkit.* She co-wrote *Buzz: The Ultimate Guide to Book Marketing* with her dear friend and mentor, Dara Beevas. After working as Marketing Director at Wise Ink Creative Publishing for almost four years, she cofounded Evergreen Authors, a website dedicated to teaching writers the business of marketing their books, in 2019.

To learn more about Evergreen Authors, visit evergreenauthors.com.

To contact Roseanne and receive a coupon code for one of her marketing courses, send her a note at roseanne@evergreenauthors.com.

Made in the USA
Middletown, DE
29 January 2021